D1671354

Women on the Move

Women on the Move: Refugees, Migration and Exile

Edited by

Fiona Reid and Katherine Holden

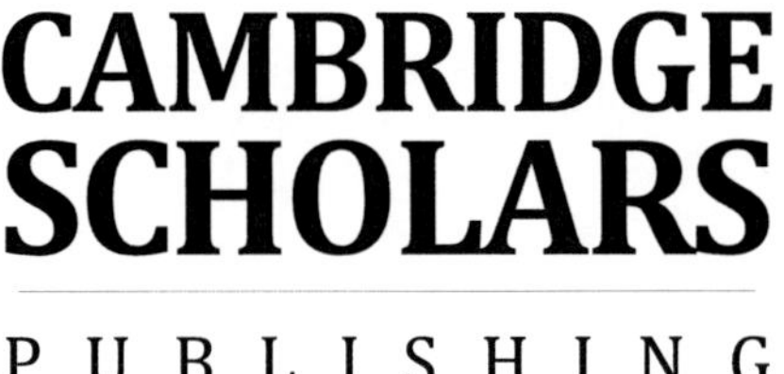

Women on the Move: Refugees, Migration and Exile,
Edited by Fiona Reid and Katherine Holden

This book first published 2010

Cambridge Scholars Publishing

12 Back Chapman Street, Newcastle upon Tyne, NE6 2XX, UK

British Library Cataloguing in Publication Data
A catalogue record for this book is available from the British Library

ISBN (10): 1-4438-2568-9, ISBN (13): 978-1-4438-2568-9

THIS VOLUME IS DEDICATED TO

TREVOR JOHNSON

URSULA MASSON

NEIL EDMUNDS

PATRICIA CLARK

ANITA HIGGIE

TABLE OF CONTENTS

ACKNOWLEDGEMENTS

This edited collection was drawn from papers presented at the thirteenth annual conference of the West of England and South Wales Women's History Network: "Women on the Move: Refugees, Migration And Exile" held at the University of the West of England (UWE) in Bristol in June 2007. We would like to thank both the UWE History Department and the Women's History Network for supporting the conference and for jointly financing the index for this book. We are also grateful to the History Departments at UWE and the University of Glamorgan for giving us time at work to edit this collection. Thanks are also due to Dr Jane Finucane for help with formatting and to committee members of the West of England and South Wales Women's History Network for general support and encouragement.

During the period between the conference and publication of this book, the editors and some of the contributors have had to cope with an unusually high number of serious illnesses and bereavements among family members and close colleagues. We have chosen therefore to dedicate the book to colleagues, partners and friends who have variously been cared for, remembered and greatly missed during these past four years.

INTRODUCTION

WOMEN ON THE MOVE

KATHERINE HOLDEN AND FIONA REID

Katerina Rancans was born in Tsarist Russia. She left the country in 1919 with her grandmother and during the interwar years she lived in Constantinople, Naples, Oporto, Bordeaux and Riga. She later married a Latvian although she always insisted that she had never given up her Russian nationality. During the war she did her best to avoid both Soviet and Nazi armies, and eventually ended up in the British zone of Germany. There she found some material security but worried endlessly about her son. "Her heart yearned that the seven-year-old Artur should have a respectable education. 'He'll be just like me, a vagabond!' she said, weeping despairingly into a handkerchief."[1]

Katerina Rancans' story contains many of the tropes we associate with female migration: loneliness, desperation, a fear of physical, masculine power, an inability to bring up children properly. The lack of a home is always painful, and possibly it is seen as being even more painful for women, given the strong cultural associations between women, mothering and home-making. Certainly women on the move are more likely to have dependants than men in similar circumstances. Rancans' life was shaped by the forces of revolution and war in the twentieth century but there is something universal in her anxiety about being "a vagabond." The fear of banishment and of being outcast has long been central to notions of European civilization. Being forced to leave the city state – and face the perilous, unsafe world outside – was one of the most ruthless punishments of the ancient world.[2] Moreover it is the first, and the most severe, punishment in the Bible. In Genesis Adam and Eve are flung from Paradise and forced to wander the world in anguish: the essence of the human condition is to regain the home we lost in that first Fall from grace. Expulsion has always been one of the most extreme penalties. Late nineteenth-century Russian nobles still feared being banished to their estates, and the imperial European powers established penal colonies far from the homeland. Whether a prisoner was sent to Siberia or Australia the message was the same: you have been banished from home; you no longer belong.

This process of expulsion or banishment requires clear boundaries, and as settled communities developed throughout Europe, the boundaries marking the community from the outside world became more marked. Medieval towns and cities were walled, and during the early modern period land became increasingly enclosed. Nineteenth-century bourgeois Europe became a place in which the ownership of clearly-marked property denoted citizenship. This idea remains powerful, especially in Britain where there is a widespread aspiration to be part of a property-owning democracy. The nations that developed throughout nineteenth-century Europe became more clearly marked by legislative and bureaucratic boundaries too. European restrictions on movement became increasingly rigid after the political upheavals of 1848, and quickly came to be seen as a normal part of government activity. Britain maintained a particular commitment to the freedom of movement throughout the nineteenth century but the Alien Act of 1905 introduced a period of far stricter border controls.[3] The passport, a document once associated with Oriental despotism, became widely accepted throughout Europe during and after the First World War. To be without state papers rapidly became an impossible condition. In response, Fridtjof Nansen, the first High Commissioner for Refugees, issued the Nansen passport to key stateless groups during the early 1920s.[4] After the Second World War refugees from Eastern Europe petitioned the International Committee of the Red Cross (ICRC) for "stateless status," mainly because they were unwilling to return to homelands dominated by the Soviet Union. Yet a life of non-belonging, a life outside of a clearly defined nation-state had become impossible and the ICRC made it clear that these requests could not be considered.[5] One example of the changing nature of European peripheries will suffice. In Thackeray's *Vanity Fair*, a novel set largely in the aftermath of the Napoleonic Wars, the main characters move easily and often between Continental Europe and Britain. Such a story would seem simply unfeasible had it been set in mid-twentieth century Europe where the rigid national boundaries were overlaid by the even more unyielding boundaries of the Cold War.

Of course the refugees petitioning for "statelessness" after the Second World War were unusual. Those living outside the protection of a state have traditionally been vulnerable to persecution, with Jews and Gypsies being the most common European examples. Even our language indicates the reviled state of the outsider: the foreigner is, by definition, foreign, strange and alien. Unlike the citizen, the local or the native, the foreigner simply does not belong. A life of movement is widely seen as being unsettled, on the contrary, becoming settled is the first step towards developing community, society and civilization.[6] Whereas the "outsider" has always occupied a difficult role, this has become even more problematic in the modern period. The growth of patriotism has ensured that the nationally-defined outsider has come to be seen as essentially different and as a potential threat to the body of the nation. In addition, technological changes, especially the development of modern, industrial warfare, have resulted in massive waves of refugees and displaced people.[7] The extent of this change cannot be under-estimated: in the summer of 1945 there were about sixteen million displaced people in Western Europe alone; in western and central Europe combined there were almost thirty million homeless people.[8] The problem of displacement continued throughout the twentieth century and at the end of 2008 the UNHCR estimated that there were about twelve million stateless people in the world.[9] In the nineteenth and twentieth centuries the scale of population movement exceeded all historical precedents as people fled from wars, revolutions and environmental catastrophes.[10] In addition, the last two centuries have been marked by a rapid increase in the level of forced population movement. As Bessel and Haake have demonstrated, the forced removal of people from their homes is not new but "its occurrence across the world as a mass phenomenon is peculiarly modern."[11] Current statistics are hard to access but according to UNHCR there were approximately forty-two million forcibly displaced people worldwide at the end of 2008.[12]

Whether voluntary or forced, population movements often evoke hostility and resistance but there is also a widespread recognition of the necessity of population movement. The "imagined community" of the nation state may be stable and homogenous but the boundaries of nation states have always been porous.[13] Moreover, some movements have been associated with status, even glamour. Merchants have grown rich on the exchange of goods and services, a process which almost inevitably involves some migration; political exiles and *émigrés* – whether notables from the French revolution or key contemporary figures such as the Dalai Lama – have often seemed exotic in their exile. The universality of religion has provoked much physical movement too. Women were politically active as religious exiles in early modern Europe and later were accepted as missionaries across the world. Whereas refugees tend to be displaced and powerless, the processes of empire-building and the workings of international capitalism have encouraged movement amongst the relatively privileged. Furthermore, the status of the immigrant is not fixed, and the persecuted refugee can become part of a new and vibrant culture. Before 1917 exiled Russian socialists formed part of a dynamic anti-Tsarist community; after 1936 the exiled Spanish republicans represented the "real Spain" in stark contrast to the fraudulent dictatorship of Franco.[14] Yet whether persecuted or privileged, the immigrant tends to remain "the other," and "immigrant history is a separate history."[15]

The chapters in this volume offer insights into many of the concerns discussed above and also pose new questions. They may at first glance seem disparate in subject matter, ranging from Sharif Gemie's acute, critical dissection of autobiographical narratives told by twenty-first century Muslim women who moved from Islamic countries to the west to Virginia Bainbridge's account of the biblically inspired exile stories told by and about sixteenth century English nuns. The book also ranges widely in time and space. While the bulk of the material is focussed either on early modern Europe or in the twentieth century, the latter period includes accounts of women moving from Muslim and European countries to the USA; and we have also included a perceptive analysis by Evelyn Spratt of how an aristocratic woman from *ancien régime* France chose to perpetuate a French cultural identity in the early years of the American Republic. This article raises questions of broader significance about the intersections between gender, class, familial and national identities.

A focus on individual or small groups of women set in a broader historical context marks out most of the chapters. Raingard Esser's chapter on the recent historiography of migrating women in Early Modern Europe is an important exception, offering a valuable overview of migration literature themes, some of which can be connected to the work of our other contributors. For one of the advantages of our approach, for readers who are interested in the book as a whole, is that it enables us to make links between chapters which may not naturally seem to fit together.

One of the connecting themes across the book is the focus on elite women. Esser argues this has been a limiting factor for most early modern migration research and points to some important studies which have broken out of this mould. Yet despite this apparent limitation in subject matter, several of our authors have paused to consider the invisible "others" who are connected to their elite subjects and who are rarely given a voice. Thus, Gemie discusses his authors' maids and speculates on how differently they might have viewed the Islamic world, while Bainbridge points out the advantages for poor English female recusants who gained the opportunity to become nuns and travel abroad by being in the service of richer and more influential women. Linda Martz's chapter takes us into different territory again. She considers the appeal of an elite Canadian migrant Pentecostal preacher in Los Angeles, Aimee Semple Macpherson, not simply to comfortably-off mid-western women migrants but also in out-reach work to marginalized populations of Hispanics, African-Americans and poor people displaced by the Great Depression of the 1930s. Essays in this book also prompt us to consider the relative advantages and disadvantages of supposedly elite status. Gibbons writes of Catholic gentlewomen in early modern England. Their status clearly gave them opportunities but their political strategies were defined and limited by their roles as wives, daughters, mothers and sisters. Evelyn Spratt's work on Josephine Du Pont also highlights the limitations faced by elite women. Du Pont's determined efforts to maintain her French identity in the new American Republic indicates the restrictions on her own power. This woman, albeit privileged in many ways, was living a life which the men in her family had chosen for her.

The significance of religion is another theme which connects the chapters. Bainbridge's Brigittine nuns were in exile in the Low Countries in the same period as the English Catholic noble women whose lives Katy Gibbons reconstructs. Both groups of women were fleeing persecution from the Elizabethan Protestant church, an experience which links them to Gemie's Muslim women four centuries later, several of whom became refugees after fearing or experiencing religious persecution in their native countries. Both the sixteenth century Brigittine nuns and the migrant woman preachers in twentieth century Los Angeles drew upon Biblical prophecy and visions to legitimate their missions. The former British suffragette Christabel Pankhurst turned to religious fundamentalism using the prophecy of Christ's return while Macpherson's work was inspired by a vision that God had told her to make her home in California. The visions and miracles which inspired and legitimated the nuns' wanderings also drew on a homecoming myth. Bainbridge argues that remembering Syon, (the Abbey from which the nuns had been compelled to flee and to which they would one day return), gave them the strength to survive as a religious community, like the Israelites in Babylon. Most of the women who feature in this collection are defined by their spiritual lives: the nuns of Syon Abbey, the Catholic noblewomen of Elizabethan England, Christabel Pankhurst and Aimee Semple McPherson, the numerous articulate women currently writing about their own experiences of Islam. Du Pont's writings are an intriguing exception. As an aristocratic French woman one might have expected her to focus on the importance of Catholicism as a symbol of her *ancien régime* identity. Yet for Du Pont it is the French language and a broadly defined French "culture" which act as the key markers of identity.

All of the essays in this collection point to the difficulties of re-creating the female experience of migration. As Esser has noted, migration could sometimes be liberating and exciting, offering women opportunities for adventure and financial independence. On the other hand migration sometimes imposes tight boundaries and re-enforces socially-conservative gender roles. It is the diversity of female migrant experiences that are best captured in this collection yet we need to ask ourselves what conclusions we can draw. Esser and Gibbons express genuine frustration at the gaps in the sources which prevent them from piecing together the lives of the women in their studies. On the other hand Du Pont's highly-detailed accounts leave us with still further questions: was Du Pont's insistence upon her own "Frenchness" typical? And in what way did her sense of authentic French identity become modified during her years in America? In a sense this is the question that underlies Gemie's essay: what can we make of one woman's narrative? Or even many women's narratives? If there is no "innocent reportage" how should we respond to women's stories of migration, refuge and exile?

Taken collectively, our authors all highlight the wide range of exile experiences. This is something we need to consider given that we live in a world increasingly characterised by movement. Globalisation has led to a sense of uniformity across much of the world. "McDonaldization" has produced a wealthy international elite as well as a more rootless poor, relentlessly in search of the work opportunities offered by international finance, industry, global food production and tourism. The classic model of forced migration has remained a potent force as people flee from wars and environmental catastrophe. Recent wars in Iraq and Afghanistan have produced vast population movements; the extent of displacement produced by the 2010 floods in Pakistan has yet to be ascertained but the impact will clearly be colossal. The forced migration model does however ignore women's agency. Aid workers who have chosen to move abroad to work in education and health projects in developing countries sometimes help the women they work with to make informed choices about where and how they want to live. This may ultimately result in those same women moving away from their own cultures and communities to seek improved conditions for themselves and their families in the developed world. Yet at this time of great movement we also witness a great hostility towards movement. This is particularly the case in Western Europe and other parts of the developed world where incoming migrants are often seen as threatening the viability of the nation state, or threatening the stability of

13. For the nation State as "imagined community" see Benedict Anderson, *Imagined Communities: Reflections on the Origin and Spread of Nationalism* (London: Verso, 1991).
14. Sharif Gemie, Laure Humbert and Fiona Reid, "Shadow Double: Refugee and Citizen," *Planet: the Welsh Internationalist* 192 (December/January 2008-2009): 64.
15. Kathy Burrell and Panikos Panayi, "Immigration, History and Memory in Britain," in *Histories and Memories: Migrants and their History in Britain*, ed. Kathy Burrell and Panikos Panayi, (London: Tauris Academic Studies, 2006), 12.
16. *Refugees Magazine*, 126 "Women Seeking a Better Deal," 2 April, 2002, 6.

what has come to be seen as the natural order. In response to the political conflicts historians must emphasise the long and varied history of population movement, displacement, exile and immigration. We should also stress the particular role of women in population movement. Currently about eighty per cent of all refugees are women or children: they require our attention.[16]

Notes

1. Margaret McNeil, *By the Rivers of Babylon: A Story Based upon actual Experiences among the Displaced Persons of Europe* (Great Britain: Lincolnshire Chronicle, 1950), 67; 218.

2. Anthony Pagden, *Peoples and Empires: Europeans and the Rest of the World from Antiquity to the Present* (London: Phoenix, 2002) .

3. Michael R. Marrus, "The Uprooted: An Historical Perspective," in *The Uprooted: Forced Migration as an International Problem in the Post-War Era*, ed. Göran Rystad (Lund: Lund University Press, 1990), 52.

4. The League of Nations established the High Commission for Refugees in 1921, and the Nansen passport was awarded to White Russians escaping the new Soviet state and Armenians who had escaped from the genocide of 1915.

5. See for example, correspondence of Otto Beilke, Comité Internationale de la Croix-Rouge, Genève, G68 932 February-April 1948.

6. For comments on civilization and settlement see A. Pagden, *Peoples and Empire* esp. 1-12.

7. M.R. Marrus, "The Uprooted," in *The Uprooted*, ed. Rystad, 50-51.

8. Mark Wyman, *DPs: Europe's Displaced Persons, 1945-1951*(Ithaca and London: Cornell University Press, 1998), 17; UNRRA, *Helping the People to Help Themselves: The Story of the United Nations Relief and Rehabilitation Administration* (London: His Majesty's Stationery Office, 1944), 11.

9. United Nations High Commission for Refugees (UNHCR) 2008 Global Trends: Refugees, Asylum-Seekers, Returnees, Internally Displaced and Stateless Persons Country Data Sheets, 16 June 2009 http://www.unhcr.org/4a375c426.html (accessed May 9, 2010).

10. For the links between the growth of empire, capitalism and environmental catastrophe see Mike Davis, *Late Victorian Holocausts: El Niño Famines and the Making of the Third World* (London: New York: Verso, 2001).

11. Richard Bessel and Claudia B. Haake, *Removing Peoples: Forced Removal in the Modern World* (Oxford: Oxford University Press, 2009), 3.

12. United Nations High Commission for Refugees (UNHCR) 2008 Global Trends: Refugees, Asylum-Seekers, Returnees, Internally Displaced and Stateless Persons Country Data Sheets, 16 June 2009 http://www.unhcr.org/4a375c426.html. (accessed May 9, 2010).

CHAPTER ONE

OUT OF SIGHT AND ON THE MARGINS? MIGRATING WOMEN IN EARLY MODERN EUROPE

RAINGARD ESSER

Every reflection on women and migration still begins, as Christiane Harzig has recently observed, by stating that women have generally been ignored by migration research and that the dominant image of a migrant in history is still male, young and unconnected.[1] This lack of a gendered view on migration, which Harzig has aptly named "malestream", is for instance, still prevalent in one of the most recent, large-scale publications on the topic: an *Encyclopaedia of Migration, Integration and Minorities in Europe since the Seventeenth Century*, currently being completed by the International Institute of Migration Studies at the University of Osnabrück (Germany) in collaboration with its Dutch counterpart at the International Institute of Social History at the University of Amsterdam. The Encyclopaedia attempts to define terminologies and theories in migration history. Here, norms and concepts taken from traditional migration studies such as assimilation and integration are applied to the complex phenomenon of cultural change in migrant communities.[2] The initial introduction to the project sent out to the contributors in 2002 listed an article on "Gender" as one of the key parameters for the study. For the final version, however, the (all male) team has decided to rearrange the volume and replace the specialist articles on approaches and methodology by a lengthy introduction to terminology and concepts of migration research followed by a number of articles, firstly on migration countries and secondly on migrant groups.[3] This new introduction does not cover the category "Gender", but makes some fleeting remarks on female migrants scattered throughout the text. Of the 213 specialist articles, only ten are distinctly dedicated to female (labour) migrants – mostly in the twentieth century.

In spite of this retreat into non-gendered migration research witnessed here, migrating women as a distinct topic of historical study are becoming increasingly important, not only as subjects of investigation in their own right, but also in providing a corrective to the abovementioned single male migrant, the "uprooted" of earlier scholarship.[4] Female migrants need to be counted and accounted for, their particular migratory strategies - if they exist - need to be analysed. The female migrant experience can also support the study of a gendered perspective on migration which is still missing. It can offer important insights into experiences and perceptions of female (and male) migrants and their self-fashioning, which are at the heart of more recent research.[5] Although differences between migrating men and women have been noted, they have not yet been mapped or described systematically over an extended period of time. Researchers such as Leo Lucassen have stressed the need for such an approach.[6] In the Netherlands, with its strong research culture in migration studies, the Netherlands Organisation for Scientific Research (NOW) funded Vici-Project "Differences that make all the difference: gender and migration (the Netherlands 1945-2005)" at Leiden University has responded to this agenda. This interdisciplinary research programme, which began in September 2006, brings together recent historical and sociological research focusing on female "guestworkers" and immigrants from the former Dutch colonies to the Netherlands. It offers the first long term study on migration from a gendered perspective. Moreover, a view on the programme of the Seventh European Social Science History Conference (ESSHC) in Lisbon in February 2008 demonstrates the current interest in this area: seven sessions particularly focus on various aspects of gender and migration (mainly in the nineteenth and twentieth centuries). These developments reflect a growing awareness of and interest in the particular roles that women had in migratory processes.

The following pages try to map recent scholarship on early modern female (and, to some extent, gendered) migration with a strong emphasis on English, Dutch and German publications in the field. Possible future areas of research will be outlined. What is suggested here might be part and parcel of modern historians' approaches to the topic, but for migration historians of the early modern period, restricted by a paucity of sources - in quantity as well as in variety - a gendered perspective on migration is still in its academic infancy. The focus will be on the migration experience rather than on strategies of immigrants once they have reached their places of destination. The linear route from emigrant to immigrant to minority to indistinguishable member of the host society, which had dominated earlier migration research, has become a bit more nuanced in recent years.[7] With an increased interest in the transitional process itself, historians have started to look at the links between the "old", home-land identity and identity in the migrants' place of destination. They also look at migration as a potentially lasting experience. It has been suggested, for instance, that *émigrés* might find a stable identity within the diaspora, that is, within the expatriate community of persons sharing the same culture outside the geographical space that gave rise to that culture. Other emigrants might lose that sense of belonging and need to re-define their identity without, however, necessarily making an effort to integrate themselves into the new host society, thus becoming exiles but not immigrants. Studies into Huguenot memoirs have demonstrated convincingly how refugees from seventeenth century France constructed a self-contained world turned inward on itself. Ego-documents have shown how effectively this exile identity could shield men and women from potential dissonances of cultural encounter with others, mitigate the shocks of displacement and neutralize the consciousness of the loss. In this process, "negative" aspects of the home culture were often re-interpreted or written out of the exile identity, while "positive" values and characteristics taken from home were (over)emphasized.[8] However, these observations might not be restricted to refugees' experiences, they could possibly also be applied to other forms of migration.

The demographics of migration are notoriously difficult to assess for medieval or earlier migrants. It is, therefore, not surprising, that research on these movements is rare and that a gendered perspective is even more difficult to detect from the few sources discussing medieval men and women on the move. Recent studies in this area have particularly focused on female pilgrims, who can be described as only temporary migrants with the clear aim of returning to their places of origin.[9] Here, the changes of the physical environment of these women on the move are closely linked to their spiritual journey and are described as such.[10]

Although exact figures are certainly also missing for early modern migrants, a quick look at what material is available, for instance, for seventeenth-century Amsterdam, shows that female migration was indeed substantial. The marriage registers of the city reveal that from 1600 to 1800 144,337 women from outside the city got married in Amsterdam. In other words, twenty-one per cent of the brides registering their marriages in Amsterdam in this period were outsiders.[11] With about as many as a quarter of all women in Amsterdam remaining single, the rate of unmarried migrant women in the city must have been substantially higher.[12] Likewise, we cannot account for women coming to the city as spouses or as widows. So, again, numbers must have been considerably higher, although it seems that family migration to Amsterdam was outnumbered by immigration of single men and single women. Even in group and family migrants, which, in the early modern period, dominated the numerous waves of confessional migration within Europe and to the Americas, women participated to a larger extent than was initially suggested. A survey of householders, listing the members of the Dutch Church in Norwich in 1568, counted 314 married persons, but sizes of households varied remarkably. The list included twenty-five maidservants, whose names are not recorded, and nineteen female relatives, usually sisters, sometimes mothers of either the husband or his wife. 193 single householders were listed, of which twenty-four were run by single women, who lived either alone or, quite frequently, with their unmarried sisters. Seventeen widows (and thirty-five widowers) were also listed as heads of households.[13] By the nineteenth century, numbers of female migrants had further increased. The most intensive period of Prairie migration in the United States, for instance, in the 1840s to 1860s, saw more than forty per cent female migrants.[14] Irish migration in the nineteenth century was similar: almost fifty per cent of Irish migrants were women. The twentieth century, finally, marked the turning point for greater female migration over longer distances. Today women account for approximately half of all global migrants, while eighty per cent of refugees are female.[15]

Research into migrating women has been explored, so far, rather unevenly. Studies of nineteenth and twentieth century women on the move far outnumber research into early modern female migration.[16] This tendency reflects migration studies in general, but is further accelerated by the distinct paucity of women's voices in the early modern period. Moreover, while modern and contemporary historians of female migration can make and have often made extensive use of sources gathered "from below" such as diaries, oral history interviews, letters etc., migration research in early modern history is strongly biased towards elite groups, such as members of the aristocracy and the higher echelons of urban society and towards members of religious organizations, where women had a higher degree of literacy and also of independent agency. However, other approaches to the study of early modern migrant women have been explored quite innovatively in recent years making use of indirect sources, which were not intentionally produced to record migratory processes. These can include marriage registers, as mentioned above, but also broadsheets and ballads, woodcuts and engravings, registers of minority churches and court records. Not surprisingly, perhaps, given the relatively high literacy rates and the closely monitored structure of social institutions such as almshouses, hospitals, guilds and parishes, towns and cities in the

Netherlands often provide better insights into female migration than other parts of Europe and it is here, where research has been unfolding in recent years with an attempt to offer a "lower class" addition to our knowledge of migrant elite women. Erika Kuijpers' recent study of Amsterdam with a particular focus on poor(er) migrants, mainly from Germany, which constituted the largest group of non-Dutch immigrants in the city in the seventeenth century, has painstakingly reconstructed the female migrant experience – as far as that is possible.[17] Here, again, records of particular institutions, such as Amsterdam's uniquely generous hospitals which offered free health care and support for pregnant women, regardless of their place of birth, have been helpful in detecting motives and female migrants' life stories. Kuijpers concludes that the pull-factor of the social support from Amsterdam's institutions, but also the knowledge of established immigrant networks, attracted women of all ages and in all stages of their lives - single girls as well as widows with or without dependent children - to the city. Lotte van de Pol has used court records to reconstruct prostitution in the city as a trade of immigrant women, who constituted by far the majority of convicted prostitutes in Amsterdam from the mid-seventeenth to the mid-eighteenth century.[18]

As seen in these examples research on women, as on migrants in general, was, and still is, to some extent, dominated by historians interested in labour migration and the economic factors behind migratory processes. Researchers have assessed the role of women in adapting to, but also shaping the labour market of their host societies. Given the guild restrictions of the early modern period, a large part of this research has been and is directed towards women in domestic service, which is, it seems, again, a growth area for female migrant work.[19] Exceptions to this emphasis on non-guild work cover research into female immigrant textile workers in the Netherlands and in Italy.[20]

Traditionally labour migration has been undertaken with a view to female contributions to the labour market at their places of destination. More recently, researchers have suggested looking at migrants' places of origin and their impact on the economy and the society that they left behind. This has been done firstly to assess the economic motives behind female migration through an analysis of the economic milieu of their places of origin, but, more importantly perhaps, researchers see migration within a network of communication and mobility not only between old and new homes, but also between family members in different parts of the world.[21] The transport and media revolutions of the last one hundred years have made it increasingly easier to keep in touch with a migrant's place of origin and have also facilitated the development of networks of migrant families, whose members are often scattered across more than one country or, indeed, one continent. But this phenomenon has not been restricted to the nineteenth, twentieth and early twenty-first centuries. Lien Luu has convincingly demonstrated that Dutch migrants in the sixteenth and seventeenth centuries kept regular contact with their places of origin. They migrated without difficulty between home, their English exile, and also the Northern Netherlands when career opportunities seemed increasingly restricted in London, and incentives to migrate were created by the new economic centres in the United Provinces which particularly targeted this adaptable, and often highly skilled, workforce.[22] Similarly, Steve Murdoch has presented a highly complex system of kinship networks maintained by Scottish emigrants in early modern Europe.[23] Neither of these two studies has undertaken a distinctly gendered approach to their work. They have, however, sharpened our understanding of migration as a process which is closely related to family dynamics. A new research agenda, therefore, focuses on family and kinship relations with their gendered and generational hierarchies (on a micro level) which negotiate migration patterns in the context of cultural, social and economic criteria prevalent both in the country of origin and the country of destination of potential migrants. Overtly economic reasons for migration can have deeper, underlying motives relating to family relations such as a flight from an abusive relative, the hope of concealing an unwanted pregnancy, or family breakdown through death and divorce. Moreover, the perceived profitability of migration might not always be based on the "rational choices" of families or family members. The decision to migrate, therefore, is as much dependent on the position of the prospective migrant in her own family as on wider economic opportunities or lack thereof. This has been explored, for instance, by Ide B. O'Carroll in her work on Irish female emigrants and sexual abuse at home in the twentieth century. It has also been discussed by Lotte van de Pol in her analysis of the "lure of the big city", i.e., early modern Amsterdam, for prostitutes.[24] The life stories of these women, written down from oral testimony in court records, recurrently mention broken families, sexual abuse and the broken promises of partners as reasons for the loss of reputation and honour in their places of origin, and a subsequent drift towards prostitution and petty crime. Although, clearly, these stories were presented in a male-dominated court scenario with the aim of showing the accused women in the best possible light, they cannot be dismissed as complete fabrications. If they were to help to limit the punishment of women on trial, they needed to demonstrate credibility and we have to take these testimonies seriously.[25]

It has been argued that women's migration relies more on extended networks than that of their male counterpart. These can be family and kinship networks, but also institutions such as religious communities. Not surprisingly, therefore, research on early modern female migration has focused on religious orders and on the role of churches in facilitating both the migration process and support in the place of destination. The works of Leslie Choquette and Natalie Zemon Davis on French nuns in Canada, Andrea Knox's recent article on Irish nuns in early modern Spain and Claire Walker's study of English convents in France and in the Low Countries are examples of these female migratory networks.[26] These studies have emphasized the degree of independence that nuns could find as migrants. For lay women church membership at their place of destination was also often an important safety net, and not just in case they fell on hard times and would need financial support. As an institution their church could vouch for their honourable conduct, an aspect that was particularly important for single women who were always under the suspicion of prostitution. It is therefore, not surprising that immigrant women entered the (minority) Lutheran church in Amsterdam in larger proportions than men.[27] For a number of early modern women, the migrant experience, therefore, can be interpreted as a liberation from the dilemmas of existing gender roles at home. Frequently, women went to Amsterdam to deliver their children, left them anonymously at the city's hospital, and returned home with a seemingly untarnished reputation to pick up the lives that they had left behind. Others tried to escape shame and ostracization through the flight into the anonymity of a big city.

Migration, however, can also perpetuate existing gender roles and fix women in their place in the family. In her study of two autobiographical accounts of a Huguenot family, written independently by a mother and her daughter, Carolyn Lougee Chappell discusses the migrant experiences of expulsion, flight and exile of two members of a French aristocratic family, who both make the category of "family", the centre of their escape stories.[28] They hold on to the idea of family solidarity, although they had been deserted by the father of the family, who did not join them in their flight, and at one stage the daughter Suzanne, a teenager at the time, was separated from her mother and elder brother and was left with some of her younger siblings to fend for herself abroad. This focus on "family" might be seen as a particular interest of an aristocratic family, whose credibility and social capital rested on reputation and lineage, but popular prints depicting German immigrant women in service in Amsterdam in the seventeenth century frequently emphasize their networks and their solidarity with the families back home. This was not always presented as an asset. A popular topic of these catchpenny prints, and also of popular plays, is the young maidservant, who marries an old widower, takes over the house and invites her impoverished extended family to the city, where they are clad, fed and entertained at the expenses of the Dutch burgher.[29]

More complicated seems to be the picture of migrating women and their role within early modern armies, that is, in communities which were non-sedentary by definition and which constituted, in times such as the Thirty Years' War, a large segment of early modern life. Not only migration historians, but also New Military Historians increasingly incorporate a gendered approach to their topic. This includes notions of masculinity, but also studies on the role of women as camp-followers, combatants and officers' spouses accompanying their husbands to the battlefields of Europe. In the seventeenth century, these women made up to fifty per cent of the armies on the move. Early modern research into gender roles in these military societies has been dominated by German and German-speaking researchers. This probably reflects the geographical focus on the Holy Roman Empire and its borders in most major conflicts of the early modern period.[30] So far, a somewhat controversial picture has emerged. One camp of historians, represented by Peter Burschel and Matthias Rogg, suggests that military life was an extension of civilian life, which perpetuated and intensified traditional social norms and gender roles. Other historians, such as Bernhard Kroener, point towards the fragility of established gender relations during campaigns, where men were at constant risk of either losing their lives or becoming invalids and thus were dependent on the income of their female partners through their services as cooks, cleaners, seamstresses, nurses, pedlars or prostitutes in the camps.[31] Moreover, where women were not accompanied by a male partner, they could acquire a form of independence through their work, which was not restricted by male rules and regulations. However, as Bertold Brecht's *Mother Courage* rightly reminds us, few women got rich in wars.[32] Desperation, lack of opportunities at home and the experience of violence also formed a substantial, if not the most prominent part of the camp-followers' lives. For dishonoured and destitute women on the margins of respectable society, life in a camp could offer a niche existence which allowed them to be integrated into a group which operated on its own terms. Voices of these women are, again, few and far between. Most research in this area has been undertaken either through the use of images produced by men for largely male buyers or through male voices such as the diary of an unknown mercenary in the Thirty Years' War, published by Jan Peters.[33] This man's story, a rare voice of an ordinary soldier on campaign, reveals the dependency of the soldier on his two (consecutive) wives to keep some form of household. Women were, indeed, indispensable in that they supplied physical and psychological support in times of war and uncertainty. How the women themselves viewed their role in the camps can, so far, only be reconstructed through diaries of aristocratic women such as Maria Cordula Freiin von Prank, verwitwete Hacke, geborene Radhaupt, an officer's wife from Carinthia, who accompanied her husband to the battlefields of the seventeenth century and who clearly saw herself as a mobile housekeeper who tried to maintain the domestic standards she was used to at home.[34]

Gender roles were certainly also converted by women who disguised themselves as men and undertook active service in early modern European armies. Not surprisingly, figures of those women are notoriously difficult to obtain, but Rudolf Dekker and Lotte van de Pol have detected 120 women in armies in the Netherlands alone in the sixteenth and seventeenth centuries.[35] Their study of female transvestism in early modern Europe tried to detect the self-perception of these women, who were mostly from the lower social strata of society, and who took decisive steps to transgress their traditional gender roles mainly to escape desperate situations and destitution at home. Yet they also cited curiosity and the prospect of adventure as motives for their re-invention. Upon discovery the women had to leave, but a distinctly negative connotation of disguised women in uniform and their dismissal as unnatural became particularly prevalent only in the eighteenth century, when, in general, women were squeezed out of early modern military life.

Within the complex of "war and female migration" however, another aspect needs to be mentioned, which is particularly associated with the twentieth-century female migration experience, but could also be applied to early modern case studies. Three out of the ten articles dedicated to female migration in the abovementioned Encyclopaedia are dedicated to brides – Filipina "mail-order brides" in Europe since the 1980s and war brides after the Second World War. Subscribing to a traditional gender role offered, for instance, German women after 1945 the only opportunity to leave their war-torn country in search of a better future. Many of these women emphasized their attributed qualities as home-makers and dedicated housewives in order to attract a husband from overseas.[36] For the eighteenth century, Andrea Knox has recently demonstrated how Irish exile women in early modern Spain used their ascribed qualities as well-educated and trustworthy companions to gain positions at court and to marry into Spanish aristocratic society.[37] Further research into the marriage strategies of migrating women, based on national, regional or religious stereotypes which women could use to their advantages could certainly also be found in other early modern scenarios. The marriage strategies of Huguenots, for instance, would probably reveal to what degree these women were able to exploit the qualities ascribed to their community, not least through their own efforts to present themselves in exile in the best possible light. So far, research has focused on the self-fashioning of the groups through their historians and community leaders. A gendered approach could certainly enrich our understanding of the community in exile and the longevity of their distinct identity abroad.[38] This aspect raises further questions of a gendered migration experience, expressed in a gendered language. It is noticeable, for instance, that female interviewees asked about their migration experience to North and South America used the words "homesick" and "homesickness" which are missing from the vocabulary of male commentators. [39] Does that mean that women are more willing to express fear, anger, frustration and disappointment in the migratory experiences undoubtedly shared by large numbers of migrants? Or is it true, as Carolyn Heilbrun suggests, that "women writing their lives conceal their pain"?[40] Marie de Rochefoucauld, in her escape *mémoire* cited earlier, blends out unwanted memories. She describes the unification of her family at their place of refuge, but omits the fact that her youngest daughter, baby Therese, had been left behind in France. She does not comment on the fact that her husband had left them alone teetering on the brink of conversion to Catholicism and only joined the family eighteen months later. She does not mention any contact which she had - inevitably - with foreigners on her travels but reduces her escape story to the help and support that she received from fellow Huguenots in different parts of Europe. Her ascribed role is the role of a steadfast Christian mother. Is it, therefore, the silences that need to be analysed as much as the accounts of women writing about exile, flight and migration?

For many migrant women religion certainly provided a framework in which they could understand and describe their journeys. But even the famous Marie Guyart de l'Incarnation, a French Ursuline nun in seventeenth-century Canada, brought to life in Natalie Zemon Davis' *Women on the Margins*, admits that it was not just her vocation and her desire to do God's work overseas, but also a sense of adventure and curiosity, that had brought her to the New World. For Maria Sybilla Merian, another migrating woman again portrayed through her own writings by Natalie Zemon Davis, migration from Frankfurt firstly to the Netherlands and then to the Dutch colony of Suriname, is seen as a spiritual journey, but also as a journey to fulfil her professional desire as a scientist and artist.[41] The letters and diaries of both women also reveal a distinctly gendered view of the world around them, which was shaped by their Eurocentric perception of the world, but also by their experiences as women and as professionals - missionary and scientist - which moderated the European claims of superiority made by their male contemporaries.

A last aspect that needs to be addressed in this context covers the area of migration and memory. Can historians detect distinct commemorative strategies amongst women and if so, how do they differ from male practices? Are, perhaps, distinct life stories about female migration experiences transported through the female family line?[42] All these questions are difficult to answer for women in early modern society, but the growing interest in a gendered approach to migration history will, it is hoped, open new interpretations and new research for these women, who will hopefully no longer remain out of sight and on the margins of migration research.

Notes

1. Christiane Harzig, "Women Migrants as Global and Local Agents. New Research Strategies on Gender and Migration," in *Women, Gender and Labour Migration: Historical and Global Perspectives*, ed. Pamela Sharpe (London: Routledge, 2001), 15-28.
2. Klaus J. Bade, Pieter C. Emmer, Leo Lucassen, and Jochen Oltmer, "Migration and integration: a conceptual guideline for authors of the Encyclopaedia Migration Integration, and Minorities since the Seventeenth Century: a European Encyclopaedia." Communication from Klaus Bade and Jochen Oltmer (July 2002).
3. Communication with Jochen Oltmer (June 6, 2007) who has kindly send me the introduction and the table of content of the book. The German version of the Encyclopaedia was published in 2007. Klaus J. Bade et al., *Enzyklopädie Migration in Europa vom 17. Jahrhundert bis zur Gegenwart* (Paderborn: Munich 2007) [2nd edition 2008]. The English edition published by Cambridge University Press is scheduled for 2010.
4. Thus the title of Oscar Handlin's seminal study on migration in the United States [first published 1951]. It painted the picture of contemporary Americans as descendents of men (and women), who had cut their "Old World" European roots and formed a new society developed under the conditions of the frontier. The book was a major success and has seen various re-editions with the latest in 2002.
5. Pamela Sharpe, "Introduction: Gender and the Experience of Migration," in *Women, Gender and Labour Migration*, 1-14. Anthropologists have offered insights into migrants' multiple identities, which can be usefully applied by historians for their research. For an overview see, for instance, Caroline B. Brettell, "Theorizing Migration in Anthropology. The Social Construction of Networks, Identities, Communities and Globalspace," in *Migration Theory. Talking Across*

Disciplines, eds. Caroline B. Brettell and James Hollifield (New York; London: Routledge, 2000), 97-137.

6. Leo Lucassen, "Grensoverschrijding. Vrouwen en gender in historische migratiestudies," in *Jaarboek voor Vrouwengeschiedenis* (Gaan & Staan, 2001), 9-35.

7. For an overview on migration research, particularly in Germany see Klaus Bade, "Historische Migrationsforschung" in *Migration in der europäischen Geschichte seit dem späten Mittelalter* (IMIS Studien 20), Osnabrück 2003, pp. 21-44. For a recent overview on early modern migration research in Britain see Ian D. White, *Migration and Society in Britain 1550-1830* (Basingstoke: Palgrave MacMillan), 2000.

8. Carolyn Lougee Chappell, "'The Pains I took to Save My/His Family': Escape Accounts by a Huguenot Mother and Daughter after the Revocation of the Edict of Nantes," *French Historical Studies* 22/1 (1999): 1-64.

9. See, for instance, Andrea Rottloff, "Stärker als Männer und tapferer als Ritter," Pilgerinnen in Spätantike und Mittelalter (Mainz: Zabern, 2007).

10. Susan Signe Morrison, *Women Pilgrims in Late Medieval England. Private Piety as Public Performance* (London: Routledge, 2000). There is also an interesting and growing literature on women and the crusades: See Sabine Geldsetzer, *Frauen auf Kreuzzügen 1096-1291* (Darmstadt: Wissenschaftliche Buchgesellschaft, 2003); Christoph T. Maier, "The Roles of Women in the Crusade Movement: A Survey," *Journal of Medieval History* 30/1 (2004): 61-82.

11. Lotte van de Pol, Erika Kuijpers, "Poor Women's Migration to the City: The Attraction of Amsterdam Health Care and Social Assistance in Early Modern Times," *Journal of Urban History* 32/1 (2005): 46. See also Jan Lucassen, "Female Migrations to Amsterdam. A Response to Lotte van de Pol," in *Women of the Golden Age. An International Debate on Women in Seventeenth-Century Holland, England and Italy* eds. Els Kloek, Nicole Teeuwen and Marijke Huisman (Hilversum: Verloren, 1994), 85.

12. Lotte van de Pol, Erika Kuijpers, "Poor Women's Migration to the City," 48.

13. W. J. Charles Moens, *The Walloons and their Church at Norwich: their History and Registers, 1565-1832* (2 vols.)(Lymington: Huguenot Society of London Publications 1, 1887-1888) Vol. 2: 207-216. Although a number of historians have studied the Dutch and Walloon immigrant communities in England in recent years, none of those have incorporated a gendered approach to their topic. See, for instance, Nigel Goose and Lien. B. Luu, introduction to *Immigrants in Tudor and Early Stuart England*, eds. Nigel Goose and Lien. B. Luu, (Brighton: Sussex Academic Press, 2005), 1-40.

14. Harzig, "Women Migrants as Global and Local Agents," 17.

15. Sharpe, "Introduction. Gender and the Experience of Migration," 2; Harzig, "Women Migrants as Global and Local Agents," and the literature cited here.

16. For an overview see Sharpe, "Introduction. Gender and the Experience of Migration," 1-14.

17. Erika Kuijpers, *Migrantenstad. Immigratie en sociale verhoudingen in 17e eeuws* (Hilversum: Verloren, 2005).

18. Lotte van de Pol, *Het Amsterdams Hoerdom, Prostitutie in de zeventiende en achttiende eeuw* (Amsterdam: Wereldbibliotheek, 1996).
19. See, for instance, Janet Henshall Momsen, ed., *Gender, Migration and Domestic Service* (London: Routledge, 1999); Hilde Bras, "Maids to the City. Migration Patterns of Female Domestic Servants," *The History of the Family* 8 (2003): 217-246.
20. S.C. Regtdoorzee Greup-Roldanus, "De vrouw in een oud-Hollandsch plattelandsbedrijf", in *Fragmenten vrouwengeschiedenis*, Vol. I, ed. W. Fritschy (The Hague: M. Nijhoff, 1980), 44-56; Els Kloek, "Vrouwenarbeid aan banden gelegd? De arbeidsdeling naar sekse volgens de keurboeken van de oude draperie van Leiden, ca. 1380-1580," *Tijdschrift voor Sociale Geschiedenis* 13 (1987): 373-402. For Italy, see, for instance: Satya Datta, *Women and Men in Early Modern Venice* (Aldershot: Ashgate, 2003).
21. See, for instance, Monica Boyd, "Family and Personal Networks in International Migration, Developments and New Agendas," *International Migration Review* 23 (1989): 689-671; Ilse Lenz et al. eds., *Crossing Borders, Shifting Boundaries*, Vol. II. *Gender and Networks* (Opladen: Leske and Budrich 2002).
22. Lien Bich Luu, Immigrants and the Industries of London, 1500-1700 (Aldershot: Ashgate, 2005).
23. Steve Murdoch, *Network North: Scottish Kin, Commercial and Covert Associations in Northern Europe, 1603-1746* (Leiden: Boston: Brill, 2006).
24. Ide B. O'Carroll, "Breaking the Silence from a Distance: Irish Women Speak of Sexual Abuse," in *Irish Women and Irish Migration*, Patrick O'Sullivan, ed., (London: Leicester University Press, 1995), 192-200; Lotte van der Pol, *Het Amsterdams Hoerdom, Prostitutie in de zeventiende en achttiende eeuw.*
25. For a discussion on the value of court records of women see Ulinka Rublack, *The Crimes of Women in Early Modern Germany* (Oxford: Clarendon Press, 1999).
26. Natalie Zemon Davis, *Women on the Margins. Three Seventeenth-Century Lives* (Cambridge, Mass.; London: Harvard University Press, 1995), 63-139; Leslie Choquette, "'*Ces Amazones du Grand Dieu*': Women and Mission in Seventeenth Century Canada," *French Historical Studies* 17/3 (1992): 627-655; Andrea Knox, "Women of the 'Wild Geese': Irish Women, Exile and Identity in Spain, 1750-1775," *Immigrants and Minorities* 23/2-3 (2005): 143-159; Claire Walker, *Gender and Politics in Seventeenth Century English Convents in France and the Low Countries* (Basingstoke: Palgrave MacMillan, 2003); See also Pascal Majérus, "Nuns in Exile? Anglo-Irish Convents in the Low Countries in the Seventeenth and Eighteenth Centuries," *History of Women Religious* (Marquette University, Milwaukee 2001) and Francis Young, "Mother Mary More and the Exile of the Augustinian Canonesses of Bruges in England, 1794-1802," *Recusant History* 27/1 (2004):86-102.
27. Kuijpers, Migrantenstad. 104-117.
28. Chappell, "'The Pains I took to Save My/His Family,'" 1-64.

29. See, for instance, the print: "Ziet hier o jonge jeugt, en merkt hoe't Westfaalse Geesje haar" in Amsterdam heeft gedragen, Gemeentearchief Amsterdam, reproduced in: Kuijpers, Migrantenstad, 194-195. See also the popular play: *De Stiefmoer* (1684) by Thomas Asselijn who uses the same stereotypes.
30. Given the prominence of Dutch armies in this conflicts and the Dutch interest in migration studies, it seems surprising that very little research has been done to understand the female experience of Dutch camp-followers. Here, reservations against what are perceived as "militaristic" topics are still quite prevalent within the Dutch academic community. See D.J.B. Trim, "Army, Society and Military Professionalism in the Netherlands during the Eighty Years' War," in *The Chivalric Ethos and the Development of Military Professionalism*, ed. D.J.B. Trim (Leiden: Boston: Brill, 2003), 269-291.
31. This area of research has been most fruitfully explored by German historians. For a general overview see Karen Hagemann, "Militär, Krieg und Geschlechterverhältnisse. Untersuchungen, Überlegungen und Fragen zur Militärgeschichte der Frühen Neuzeit," in *Klio in Uniform? Probleme und Perspektiven einer modernen Militärgeschichte der Frühen Neuzeit*, ed. Ralf Proeve (Cologne; Weimar; Vienna: Böhlau, 1997), 35-88. For Irish female migration and war: Gráinne Henry, "Women 'Wild Geese', 1585-1625: Irish Women and Migration to European Armies in the Late Sixteenth and Early Seventeenth Centuries," in *Irish Women and Irish Migration*, 23-40.
32. Bertold Brecht, *Mutter Courage und ihre Kinder* (1939) [first printed 1949].
33. Bernhard Kroener, "'…und ist der jammer nit zu beschreiben'. Geschlechterbeziehungen und Überlebensstrategien in der Lagergesellschaft des Dreißigjährigen Krieges," in *Landsknechte, Soldatenfrauen und Nationalkrieger. Militär und Geschlechterordnung im historischen Wandel*, eds. Karen Hagemann and Ralf Pröve (Frankfurt: Campus Fachbuch, 1998), 279-297; Matthias Rogg, *Landsknechte und Reisläufer: Ein Stand in der Kunst des 16. Jahrhunderts* (Paderborn: Schöningh Ferdinand Gmbh, 2002); Jan Peters, *Ein Söldnerleben im Dreißigjährigen Krieg. Eine Quelle zur Sozialgeschichte* (Berlin: Akademie-Verlag 1993).
34. "Gedenkbuch der Frau Maria Cordula Freiin von Pranck, verwitwete Hacke, geb. Radhaupt, 1595-1700," printed in: *Steiermärkische Geschichtsblätter* 2, (1881) H.1: 9-29. For further comments on this source see also Heide Wunder, *"Er ist die Sonn,' sie ist der Mond". Frauen in der Frühen Neuzeit* (Munich: Beck, 1992), 18-19.
35. Rudolf Dekker and Lotte van de Pol, *The Tradition of Female Transvestism in Early Modern Europe* (Basingstoke: Palgrave MacMillan, 1989).
36. Raingard Esser, "'Language No Obstacle': War Brides in the German Press, 1945-1949," *Women's History Review* 12/4 (2003): 577-604.
37. Knox, "'Women of the Wild Geese,'" 143-159.
38. Etienne François, "Die Traditions- und Legendenbildung des deutschen Refuge," in *Der Exodus der Hugenotten. Die Aufhebung des Ediktes von Nantes 1685 als europäisches Ereignis* , ed. Heinz Duchhardt (Cologne: Böhlau, 1985), 177-185.

39. See *Neue Illustrierte* (26 May 1949) see also: *Neue Illustrierte* (27 February and 26 March 1952).
40. Carolyn Heilbrun, *Writing a Woman's Life* (New York: Ballantine Books, 1988) cited in Louge Chappell, "'The Pains I took to Save My/His Family,'" 9.
41. Natalie Zemon Davis, *Women on the Margins*, 140-202.
42. On these issues see Carolyn Lougee Chappell, "'What's in a Name?': Self Identification of Huguenot *Réfugiées* in Eighteenth-Century England," in *From Strangers to Citizens: The Integration of Immigrant Communities in Britain, Ireland and Colonial America 1550-1750,* eds. Randolph Vigne and Charles Littleton (London: Sussex Academic Press, 2001), 539-548.

CHAPTER TWO

PROPAGANDA AND THE SUPERNATURAL: THE BRIDGETTINE NUNS OF SYON ABBEY IN EXILE, C.1539-1630

VIRGINIA BAINBRIDGE

Syon Abbey was the most prestigious monastic community founded in later medieval England.[1] It was the only English house of *Bridgettines*, an order of women contemplatives, founded by St. Bridget of Sweden (1303-1373).[2] An outspoken member of the Swedish royal family, St. Bridget used her considerable force of personality to expose and condemn the corruption of world leaders, both religious and secular, and to advocate Church reform and world peace. The prayers of her strictly enclosed nuns were considered powerful because of their austere lifestyle and they were served by a college of priests who promoted St. Bridget's reformist agenda.[3]

Syon Abbey is renowned for its lavish foundation by King Henry V in 1415 and its patronage by Lancastrian, Yorkist and Tudor royal dynasties. The community was a centre of the Humanist reform favoured at court during Henry VIII's marriage to Katherine of Aragon, and was associated with the political faction which lost ascendancy over his divorce, his marriage to Anne Boleyn and his supremacy over the English church.[4] Despite being royal servants, the community placed conscience over duty to the monarch and its continuing loyalty to Rome placed Syon at the forefront of political and religious opposition to the Tudor state. Like St. Thomas More and other leading conservatives, Syon supported Elizabeth Barton, the Holy Maid of Kent, a political prophetess in the mould of St. Bridget, executed in 1534 for prophesying doom to Henry VIII if he married Anne Boleyn.[5] The price of this support was the martyrdom of Syon priest St. Richard Reynolds at Tyburn in 1535.[6] His speech to the tribunal which sentenced him to death and his dying words from the scaffold won a propaganda victory for the supporters of Rome.[7] Syon featured in propaganda from both sides of the emerging religious divide.

Anne Boleyn was said to have visited the nuns in 1534, they met her with passive disobedience and a refusal to accept reformist literature, although this may have been a Protestant rumour spread to discredit the Bridgettines.[8] Friar William Peto, a confessor of Katherine of Aragon, cast Henry VIII as the wicked biblical King Ahab, and by implication, Anne Boleyn as his wife Jezebel.[9] Peto's prophecy of 1535 was said to have come true in 1547 when Henry's corpse, lying at Syon overnight, exploded in its coffin and dogs were found licking up his remains, the fate which befell Ahab.[10]

Syon Abbey played a significant role in forging English Roman Catholic identity in the later sixteenth and early seventeenth centuries. Small but determined numbers of women made the journey into exile to follow their vocations at Syon, the only English-speaking house of nuns from 1539 to 1598. They endured uncertainty, poverty and danger in the Low Countries and Northern France. They were driven from place to place by the Religious Wars and in 1594 they finally fled to Lisbon, a port in Spanish territory. This was an era of fierce propaganda battles between English Protestant and Catholic factions and international political interests. According to official Protestant dogma the age of miracles was over but the seductive appeal of Roman Catholicism was that it continued to authenticate believers' experience of the supernatural in their daily lives.[11] The Bridgettines lived marginal lives as refugees, but their mediation of the divine through prayer, relics and miracles enhanced their status in their host communities.[12] They interpreted their exile and wanderings in biblical terms and this gave them the strength to survive as a religious community, like the Israelites in Babylon remembering Syon.[13]

The First Exile and Return to England

Following the martyrdom of Richard Reynolds, Syon's fall from royal favour continued. The Brothers and Sisters maintained their opposition to Henry VIII's religious policies with few exceptions.[14] In 1537, lay Brother Thomas Brownell died of fever in the squalid conditions of Newgate Jail, a common death for sixteenth-century Roman Catholic martyrs.[15] Although Syon reached an uneasy truce with the government, it was dissolved with the other larger monasteries in 1539.

In 1539 Abbess Agnes Jordan (d. 1544) and her nuns left their home at Isleworth, Middlesex, for an uncertain future. Later they claimed that their community was never dissolved because they chose not to hand in their convent seal or the keys to their house. Some of the fifty-six Sisters and seventeen Brothers were placed under house arrest where their activities could be monitored, and others retired in groups to live, according to the

Rule, with relatives who were wealthy enough to accommodate them.[16] Agnes Jordan supported a large group on her substantial pension of £200 a year, at Southlands, a house rented from Edmund Peckham at Denham, Buckinghamshire.[17] Syon's Brothers were shared out among the groups of Sisters to provide access to the sacraments. As far as possible the community was organised and ready to return home to Syon as soon as religious policies allowed.

Sister Catherine Palmer emerged as the leader of a group which joined the exodus of Catholic intellectuals leaving England in 1539.[18] Few details of this first phase of Syon's exile are known, but her group first found refuge with the Augustinian canonesses at Antwerp, known as the Falcon Sisters.[19] On Agnes Jordan's death in 1544, Catherine Palmer returned to collect those who had lived with her and the enlarged group went to live with their fellow Bridgettines at the abbey of Mariatroon at Dendermonde (Termonde), Flanders. In 1553 Mariatroon received a visit from the young Mary, Queen of Scots (1542-87), who began an intermittent association with Syon.[20]

By 1556 Queen Mary Tudor had successfully returned England to Roman Catholicism and leading religious exiles, including the Bridgettines, were recalled. They stayed with the Falcon Sisters at Antwerp once again while they were waiting to embark for England.[21] In 1557, eighteen Sisters and three Brothers, around one third of those pensioned eighteen years before were solemnly re-enclosed at Isleworth under Abbess Palmer.[22] Syon was apparently recruiting other exiled nuns through English networks in the Low Countries, as a place was reserved for Sister Elizabeth Woodford, a scholarly nun professed at Burnham Abbey in 1519. After Burnham Abbey was dissolved in 1538, Sister Elizabeth retired to the household of Dr John Clement and his wife Margaret (née Giggs), St. Thomas More's ward. At the start of Edward VI's reign Clement took his household into exile at Louvain and in 1548 Sister Elizabeth entered the Flemish-speaking convent of St. Ursula's where she was later joined by the Clements' daughter Margaret, a future prioress, and twenty-five other English women. Sister Elizabeth decided against returning to England in 1557.[23] Abbess Catherine Palmer and her Sisters did not remain at Syon for long. Queen Mary's death on 17th November 1558 was recorded in the Syon Martiloge, and in May 1559 Queen Elizabeth suppressed the few re-founded religious communities.[24] England's return to Protestantism left the Bridgettines no choice but to return to exile in the Low Countries, if they were to continue their shared contemplative life.

Exile in the Low Countries

The Spanish ambassador, Gomez, Duke of Feria (d.1571) arranged passports and chartered a ship to carry the Bridgettines, the Carthusian monks of Sheen, the Dominican nuns of Dartford and other Roman Catholic refugees into exile.[25] His family history shows how patronage of Syon was passed down through several generations and contributed to the community's survival in exile. The Duke was married to Jane Dormer (1538-1612), a lady of Queen Mary's court.[26] Jane's great-aunt was Sister Mary Newdigate of Syon (d. 1535) whose brother Sebastian, once a courtier and friend of Henry VIII, became a Carthusian monk after his wife died.[27] Sebastian's refusal to acknowledge royal supremacy over the Church led to his martyrdom in 1535, he was allegedly singled out for harsh treatment because Henry felt betrayed by his former friend.[28] Their sister Lady Joanna Dormer (d. 1571), supported leading Catholic intellectuals under Edward VI, and these were later promoted by Queen Mary. In exile, she was a benefactor of the University of Louvain and of Syon. Her son William Dormer was a member of Queen Mary's council. William and his wife Mary, the daughter of Sir Henry Sidney a prominent courtier, were Jane's parents. Her cousin Sir Philip Sidney (1554-86), was among the officers of English troops who protected the Syon nuns from Calvinist soldiers at Mechlin in the 1570s.[29] On her progress to Spain Jane became close to Mary Queen of Scots, and at the Spanish court she was a leading supporter of English, Scottish and Irish Roman Catholicism.[30] Her two great-nieces, Anne (Bridget in religion) and Lucy, daughters of Anthony Maria Browne, the second Viscount Montagu and the most powerful English Catholic of his generation, became nuns at Syon in the early seventeenth century.[31]

The experience of the Bridgettines in the Low Countries paralleled the experience of their fellow-travellers the Carthusians, and the Dominicanesses: they all commenced a period of "wanderings" which lasted for decades.[32] Their poverty and the dangers of the Religious Wars made it impossible for them to settle permanently. Initially the Bridgettines returned to Mariatroon at Dendermonde and the two communities, one English and the other Flemish, lived side-by-side under two abbesses. Inevitably pressure on living space, lack of money and issues of authority led to tensions.[33] Syon remained at Mariatroon for about four years relying on a small pension from Philip II of Spain, alms from other religious exiles and money from their families at home.[34] The outbreak of the Religious Wars made its position dangerous and so in 1563 Philip II's regent, Margaret of Parma, placed Bethany, an abandoned *béguinage* at the community's disposal. This lay at Hemstede near Zurich Zee in the province of Zeeland.[35] Because the low-lying site was unhealthy, Dr Nicholas Sander (c. 1530-1581) the Roman Catholic apologist and brother of Sisters Margaret and Elizabeth Sander, bought the monastery of *Mons Pacis* (Mount Peace) and its lands from the Augustinians of Mishagen in 1567.[36] This became Syon's home between 1568 and 1571 and the community, which numbered twenty-two in 1569, re-established religious life there, praying for the Augustinians' benefactors as well as their own. *Mons Pacis* lay at Eeckeren in the countryside outside Mishagen, near the port of Antwerp. Antwerp was at the centre of fierce fighting and the monastery's isolated position made it vulnerable to attack. The Bridgettines experienced regular harassment by Calvinist and Lutheran troops, and in 1571 they were forced to take refuge in Antwerp. [37]

From Antwerp they made their way south to Mechlin (Malines), where they lived from 1572 for around seven years.[38] Sir Francis Englefield helped the Bridgettines to rent a substantial house with gardens on *la Rue du Vieux-Bruul* near the Butter Market.[39] Englefield was one of the leaders of the English exile community.[40] He had been a member of Queen Mary's Council and his extended family included several generations of patrons and inmates of Syon. The Bridgettines came to Mechlin during one of its most troubled periods. Serious fighting between Catholic and Protestant forces ceased just before they arrived in 1572.[41] In 1576 townsmen searching for soldiers and weapons broke into the convent, violated the enclosure and looted its goods. The mob was met by the aged Abbess Catherine Palmer at the head of her community: she never recovered from the shock and died soon afterwards.[42] The town authorities also confiscated two-thirds of the annual Spanish pension of £600. In a diplomatic move that same year, Philip II revoked the pensions of exiled religious and expelled many English exiles. As a result of these events, the Bridgettines sank deeper into poverty necessitating desperate measures.[43] In 1578 the new Abbess, Bridget Rooke, was forced to break up the community by sending the younger sisters from well-connected families back to England to collect alms and to shelter until community life could be fully restored.[44] Renewed hostilities broke out and there was widespread destruction in the suburbs. The rest of the community was forced to abandon life at Mechlin in 1580. They left for Antwerp under an escort of English soldiers from the army of the Prince of Orange and embarked by ship for Rouen.[45]

Recruiting Bridgettines

It is clear from this brief account of Syon's years in the Low Countries that religious life there was unpredictable and dangerous. Nevertheless, young English recruits continued to be drawn to the Bridgettines, in preference to the Dominicanesses, whose community numbered twelve, mainly elderly, members in 1559 and died out in 1585.[46] In 1587 Syon Abbey had twenty-four Sisters and six Brothers, a total of thirty members, and thirty-one in 1594 when there were twenty-three Sisters and eight Brothers.[47] What made English gentry women leave their homes to become nuns in exile? John Gee's pamphlet *New Shreds of the Old Snare* satirised the process by which they came to realise their vocation: unscrupulous priests and Jesuits interested in their money played on their emotions and convinced them to rely on the guidance of supernatural visions, then spirited them away through an underground network of contacts to join religious orders on the Continent.[48] This parodies the experience of the daughters of Sir John Arundel (d. 1590), whose household was served by the charismatic priest Father John Cornelius, a contemplative credited with supernatural powers.[49] The sisters' Anglican half-brother John, the ninth Lord Stourton (d.1588) appeared to Cornelius when he was saying mass for his soul, begging for his family's prayers from Purgatory.[50] Others present, including Dorothy Arundel, also experienced manifestations. Cicely Arundel (d. 1623), had become a Bridgettine by 1587 and Cornelius reminded Dorothy of her own vow to St. Bridget when he wrote to her on the eve of his martyrdom in 1594. Instead, she and her sister Gertrude entered the English Benedictine house of Brussels when it was founded in 1598.[51]

The Life and Good End of Sister Marie, a contemporary biography of Sister Mary Champney of Syon (d. 1580), tells a similar story from a nun's perspective.[52] The manuscript was based on Mary's own reflections as she lay dying of tuberculosis. She went abroad in the 1560s as a "waiting gentlewoman with one of good worship" and was placed with nuns at Antwerp to study Latin and the Divine Office. At first she was homesick, but following a crucial vision at Mass and with the support of local Jesuits, she decided to stay in Flanders and become a nun. During her period of training her friends took her to visit the Bridgettines at Meshagen. Their distinctive habit reminded her of a vision she received aged twelve, and she understood that this was the order for which she was destined. She was professed in 1569 and was Chantress by 1572. She was one of the younger nuns sent back to England for safety in 1578 and to help raise funds, when the community was approaching starvation.

Suffering from advanced tuberculosis aggravated by conditions at Syon, she spent her last weeks at a Catholic safe house at Fulham. This final period of her life coincided with Lent and Easter-tide and her faith inspired her many visitors. Her funeral was a major gathering of recusants, celebrated by a college of priests.

The way in which recruits like Mary Champney reached Syon and other English-speaking nunneries founded after 1598 follows a common pattern. English recusants, especially poorer ones, gained the opportunity to travel abroad in the households of wealthy and influential persons. When the widowed Grace, Lady Babthorpe entered the religious life at St. Ursula's Augustinian convent, Louvain, she brought her maid Ursula Whitseal with her and later helped two more servants, Ann and Mary Stonehouse, to become nuns.[53] The household of Syon's patron, the widowed Jane, Duchess of Feria was run on semi-monastic lines, and one or two servants left each year to join various religious orders.[54] Her great-nieces Anne (Bridget) and Lucy Browne were accompanied to Syon by their maid Anne.[55]

The Making of Syon's History in Rouen

For women like Margaret Woodford and Mary Champney, performance of the Divine Office, study and contemplation were the central activities of their religious life.[56] When Syon left the Low Countries for Rouen in 1580, having sold the property at Meshagen, the luggage the community registered with the port authorities for the voyage comprised of two great and two small casks and a great barrel all containing books, five more containers of unbound books and an enormous package of altar pieces.[57]

At Rouen the Bridgettines were welcomed by John Leslie, exiled Bishop of Ross and former secretary to Mary Queen of Scots, who was to be one of their chief supporters during their fourteen years in France.[58] Unfortunately, they had travelled from one region blighted by civil war to another. The French Wars of Religion had begun in 1562 and were to continue until 1594. Rouen, like Antwerp, was a major port and economic centre and thus of strategic importance. The Bridgettines lived through two sieges of Rouen, one in 1589 and one in 1591-92, and both mounted by Anglo-French forces.[59] Both Bishop Leslie and Father Forster, Syon's confessor-general, supported the Catholic League defeated by Henry IV in 1593 and this necessitated Syon's flight to Lisbon in the Spanish territory of Portugal in 1594.

A History of Syon's Wanderings is the main source on Syon's exile.[60] Several versions were developed at Rouen by members of the community and their supporters for propaganda purposes. The account organised a fractured history into a coherent narrative around the theme of exile, thus identifying Syon with Israel, God's chosen people of the Old Testament. It highlighted certain themes including the vulnerability of Catholic womanhood as fighting forced the Sisters to move from place to place, their poverty and the support of wealthy benefactors. Potential benefactors were clearly an intended audience. It emphasised the supernatural guidance the Bridgettines received through dreams and visions as they moved towards their destiny and it provides a unique window into their mental world in the decades around 1600. The mythology of Syon's wanderings was created by Father Forster, Syon's confessor-general from 1584 to his death in 1628, assisted by leading exiles, Father Robert Persons the Jesuit, and Sir Francis Englefield.[61] A longer version was written by one of the Bridgettine Brothers or Sisters once the community was settled at Lisbon.[62]

The *History* discreetly ignored the majority of nuns who continued their monastic lives in England between 1539 and 1559. It focused instead on the group which went into exile under Catherine Palmer, linking Syon's sufferings abroad with the experience of hard-line English Catholics who chose exile rather than compromise the practice of their faith, or who sought exile of necessity because of their political acts and allegiances. They and their supporters in England were an intended audience of the narrative which centred on Father Forster, who shared this background.[63] Father Seth alias Joseph Forster (d. 1628) came from a prominent Yorkshire gentry family which produced a number of martyrs. He was well-educated, well-connected and politically astute, all qualities which were vital to Syon's survival in the late 1500s and early 1600s. His parents and Isabel, the wife of his elder brother William, all died while imprisoned for recusancy in York Castle in the early 1580s. William died later in exile at Antwerp and several of his children followed religious vocations, perhaps out of financial necessity as much as choice. Two became Jesuits, Seth and Thomas, a missionary who died in Lincoln gaol, and Clare Dowman alias Forster (d. 1627) was professed at Syon in 1609. Two of her Syon contemporaries, Sister Frances Holtby (fl. c. 1610-22) and Sister Anne Wharton (d. 1632) were probably her cousins. Clare's eldest brother Richard Forster (c. 1585-1661) was a Roman Catholic courtier of Henrietta Maria and Charles I.[64] Father Forster himself studied at Douai, he was one of the students Cardinal Allen sent to found the English College at Rome and he received a pension from the Pope. Forster helped the Bridgettines to find a home in Rouen in 1584 after all of Syon's Brothers had died. Having been persuaded to become confessor-general, he recruited a new body of Brothers and secured some patronage from the King of France. Following the second siege of Rouen he arranged Syon's passage to Portugal and negotiated a pension from the King of Spain. In Lisbon he developed good relations with English merchants and his nephew, Richard Forster, helped him to recruit new members for Syon.

An early chapter of the *History* recounts Forster's near death from alleged poisoning when he was Syon's only priest, and his miraculous recovery.[65] He was already given up as dead and prayers were being offered for his soul in English seminaries when Sister Gertrude Tyrrell was given a sign that his life would be spared. As she prayed earnestly before an image of Our Blessed Lady, her candle was extinguished as if he had died and the flame miraculously re-lit to indicate his recovery. As a person of holy life, Gertrude's prayers were considered powerful and she became a channel through which the divine will was revealed to her community.

At Rouen, poverty continued to be a major problem despite the generosity of some leading citizens and English exiles. In 1587, *A supplication made for poore Syon,* an early version of the *History* was addressed to "all charitable and well-disposed Catholics on behalf of the religious virgins and brethren of Syon."[66] The document summarised the wanderings of the community under Abbesses Catherine Palmer and Bridget Rooke, and it begged for alms in order to avert its dissolution. It was signed by twenty-four Sisters headed by Abbess Rooke, including Elizabeth Sander, who had recently returned from imprisonment in England, and six Brothers headed by Father Forster. Numbers were replenished by a steady flow of recruits from families of Roman Catholic activists.[67] Prioress Ursula Hoorde (d. 1598), came from a family which belonged to the pre-Reformation intellectual and clerical elite and she and her cousin William Hoorde were heavily involved in Roman Catholic resistance to Elizabeth's regime.[68] William was imprisoned with Sister Elizabeth Sander in 1580 for distributing Campion's *Challenge* and later he helped her to escape. Jane Wiseman, who took her children to visit the Roman Catholic prisoners in the notorious Wisbech gaol and was later condemned to death for treason, was the mother of Anne (d. 1650) and Barbara (d. 1649) Wiseman who both became abbesses of Syon.[69] Such women were propelled into exile by their family's ideology. Others, like Father Forster and his relatives, were refugees fleeing from the effects on their families of martyrdom and persecution. The *Supplication* was obviously successful in attracting funds as Syon survived, although in very difficult conditions.

In one of her letters to her kinsman Sir Francis Englefield, Elizabeth Sander vividly described the suspicion the community lived under and the very real possibility of the Brothers' execution as English-speaking traitors within Rouen. Syon was searched for concealed weapons, accused of destroying the city's water conduits when the convent was flooded, and of spreading the plague.[70] The *History of Syon's Wanderings* recorded situations when God intervened miraculously: the preservation from death of a Brother from a canon ball and of Father Forster from a chain shot, were "two special favours of God," and when the authorities failed to find provisions when searching the enclosure, the Bridgettines interpreted this as "the manifest finger of God" preserving their precious rations.[71] Their prayers, their church, a place of refuge which held relics including a piece of the true cross given by Queen Mary Tudor, and miracles attributed to St. Bridget, all considerably raised the esteem in which the community was held in such troubled times and attracted patronage from influential citizens.[72] The *History* describes three miracles of St. Bridget.[73] A public notary experienced an "amazing miracle wrought by our holy mother St. Bridget," when a candle set his papers on fire one evening and he called out to her and the flames were immediately extinguished. In gratitude he gave the community alms, free legal advice indefinitely and a stained glass window painted with an image of the Holy Trinity. Around the same time, a pilot who had witnessed the devotion of the people in the convent church, invited his ship's company to call upon St. Bridget when they were caught in a dangerous storm and had lost all hope of escape. After the tempest ceased and they found themselves in safety he collected alms and sent them to the Bridgettines with a record of the miracle. In the third miracle, Captain Pedrier in the thick of fighting at the Battle of Dreux, was in grave danger of being killed, but miraculously escaped by vowing a silver lamp to St. Bridget, which he placed in the convent church.

By the time the Abbess Bridget Rooke died on the feat of the Epiphany in 1594, the Bridgettines had achieved a measure of respect in Rouen. The Abbess's funeral was well-attended by people of all ranks, including members of the Court of Parliament, and her body was accompanied by her Bridgettine brethren, the four orders of friars, and twelve virgins dressed in white, each carrying a white taper, organised by a wealthy lady benefactor.[74] The funeral was conducted by the Bishop of Ross and the Cathedral theologian preached the sermon. The *History* recorded the effect of exile on this woman, who died after a long sickness, worn out by travels and troubles, and heart-broken by poverty and the break-up of the community in Flanders. Her life as a religious woman in exile was described in paradoxical terms: she was a captain or general who led her company through terrible events, a pattern of humility to all though a superior, an example of the greatest mildness though a governor and corrector. Father Forster considered her prayers so powerful that they caused him to enter Syon.[75] He sought her interpretation of a disturbing dream which seemed to foretell the need to leave France.[76] When the community was praying for guidance about where to go, she appeared to him in a dream, and was a comfort "knowing her great affection to him and that convent and that she certainly prayed and used all her interest with Our Lord for us in these great dangers."[77]

From Rouen to Lisbon

The whole process of travelling from Rouen to Lisbon over Easter 1594 was guided "by the divine help and providence of God," a necessity given the lack of information for such a voyage in hostile military conditions.[78] Earlier that year, Queen Elizabeth's physician Dr Rodrigo Lopez, a Portuguese Jew and double agent, was condemned to death for plotting to poison her. Hostile factions hampered the journey, believing the community's hurried departure from Rouen and choice of Portugal as their destination revealed their involvement in this notorious plot.[79] Father Forster called on St. Bridget, an experienced traveller and pilgrim, for guidance and received a series of dreams: he saw weapons of war turned into instruments of the passion, he wrestled with the devil and heard him say "now I will be revenged of thee presently," causing them to lose their ship at Newhaven and many other problems.[80] He later heard a voice singing of Israel's delivery from Egypt, meaning that the Devil's power had been broken by the prayers of the English Capucins; and afterwards he discovered that God had sent fog to protect their ship from capture by four English men-of-war.[81]

The reception Syon received in Lisbon was mixed, reflecting the uncertainties of exile.[82] They were greeted warmly by the archbishop, but later experienced difficulty having the Bridgettine Rule recognised by the diocesan authorities. There were the usual problems of finding suitable accommodation for an enclosed religious order on very little money and of attracting new patrons. However, by the 1620s, Syon was well established at Lisbon and Father Forster was repositioning the Bridgettines for a possible return from exile after the death of James I. Syon's patrons Anthony Browne, Viscount Montagu in England, and his aunt Jane, Duchess of Feria in Spain, were leading supporters of a marriage between the future Charles I and the Spanish Infanta, hoping it would lead to toleration for Roman Catholics in England.[83] Forster commissioned an illuminated manuscript of the *History of Syon's Wanderings* as a gift for the Infanta, emphasising Syon's foundation by King Henry V of England and its protection by the King of Spain.[84]

Thomas Robinson's scurrilous pamphlet, *The Anatomy of the English Nunnery at Lisbon*, was first printed in 1622 and reprinted several times in the 1620s and 1630s, a time of heightened anxiety about Roman Catholicism in England.[85] The author claimed to have been a novice Brother at Syon but the account may have been merely Protestant propaganda. Syon was part of the Counter-Reformation resurgence of English monasticism and Father Forster was well-placed to play a significant role in English politics. The author had little to report, but implied that the aged father had improper relations with Abbess Preston and the nuns and that his shrewd investments in Portuguese trade supported Syon financially. More significantly, the pamphlet attacked Syon's continuing ability to recruit young nuns and priests by appealing to parental anxieties: it suggested that Syon was in the third rank, below the aristocratic foundations of the Low Countries, and even the Poor Clares.[86]

The failure of the Spanish match was not the end of Father Forster's ambition to renew Syon's special relationship with the English monarchy. Forster probably used his nephew Richard Forster to gain influence at the court of Charles I. His queen, Henrietta Maria was a devotee of St. Bridget and Richard Forster was a prominent member of her household in England and later in exile in France.[87]

Conclusion

Syon Abbey was founded to intercede on behalf of its royal patrons with God and his saints in the supernatural realm. However, the community's refusal to accept royal authority over the English church in the 1530s had severe consequences which included persecution, martyrdom and exile. Both before and after its dissolution in 1539, Syon Abbey played a significant role in the propaganda battle for hearts and minds in the English Reformation. Although they were pioneers of monastic exile, the Bridgettines have not been assessed alongside other English exile communities in the Low Countries and Northern France until recently because of their relocation to Lisbon in 1594.[88] Surviving propaganda of both the Bridgettines and their enemies from the 1580s to the 1620s reveals that Syon was still regarded by contemporaries as politically significant. The community continued to recruit postulants from

English court circles and patronage by the Kings of Spain maintained its profile. While the Spanish Infanta was the intended bride of the future Charles I, Syon seemed poised to return to its old role serving the English monarchy.

Despite Syon's ability to attract powerful patrons, its existence came at the price of poverty, near starvation and frequent homelessness for its members. For them the age of miracles was not over, and the *History of Syon's Wanderings* and their other writings testify to God's miraculous preservation of the community on its journey from England in 1539, and its subsequent journey to Lisbon in 1594.[89] Supernatural guidance was part of the daily lives of the Sisters and Brothers who received signs to determine their vocations abroad, and dreams and visions revealing God's will for the whole community. According to Psalm 137, the Israelites, in exile in Babylon, wept when they remembered Syon.[90] In exile in Lisbon for over 250 years, the Bridgettines celebrated their Englishness and their royal connections by venerating early medieval English royal saints whose portraits they commissioned for their convent.[91] The judicious use of propaganda, powerful patrons in England and abroad and extended family networks all contributed to the community's survival. Their religious faith was rewarded by God's guidance in the uncertainties of exile and on their return home to England in 1861 following Roman Catholic emancipation. After an unbroken 600 year history Syon Abbey is currently located in Devon.

Notes

I would like to thank my colleagues in the History Department at the University of the West of England for encouraging my research, especially Dr. Trevor Johnson (d. 2007).

1. George J. Aungier, *The History and Antiquities of Syon Monastery, Isleworth* (London: J.B. Nichols, 1840).
2. Bridget Morris, *St Birgitta of Sweden* (Woodbridge, Suffolk: Boydell, 1999).
3. Virginia R. Bainbridge, "Women and the Transmission of Religious Culture: Benefactresses of Three Bridgettine Convents," *Birgittiana* 1 (1997): 55-76; Virginia R. Bainbridge, "The Bridgettines and Major Trends in Religious Devotion c.1400-1600," *Birgittiana* 19 (2005): 225-240.
4. Maria Dowling, "Humanist Support for Katherine of Aragon," *Bulletin of the Institute of Historical Research* 57 (1984): 46-55.
5. Alan Neame, *The Holy Maid of Kent: the Life of Elizabeth Barton 1506-1534* (London: Hodder and Stoughton, 1971).

6. Adam Hamilton, *The Angel of Syon: the Life and Martyrdom of the Blessed Richard Reynolds* (Edinburgh: Sands, 1905); Virginia R. Bainbridge, "Reynolds, Richard" in *The Oxford Dictionary of National Biography* (hereafter *DNB*) ed. Lawrence Goldman. http://www.oxforddnb.com/view/article/23430 (accessed August 30, 2010).
7. *Calendar of Letters and Papers, Foreign and Domestic, of the Reign of Henry VIII* (London: HMSO, 1864-1932) Vol. 7, 661.
8. "William Latimer's Chronicle of Anne Bulleyne," ed. Maria Dowling, *Camden Miscellany*, Vol. XXX Series 4, 39 (London: Royal Historical Society, 1990): 23-65.
9. Dowling, "Humanist Support for Katherine of Aragon," 52-55.
10. Aungier, *Syon*, 92; Neame, *Holy Maid*, 155-57.
11. Alexandra Walsham, "Miracles and the Counter-Reformation Mission to England," *Historical Journal* 46 (2003): 779-815.
12. Trevor Johnson, "Blood, Tears and Xavier Water: Jesuit Missionaries and Popular Religion," in *Popular Religion in Germany and Central Europe, 1400-1800*, eds. Bob Scribner and Trevor Johnson (London, MacMillan, 1996), 183-202.
13. *The Bible*, Psalm 137.
14. Aungier, *Syon*, 83-88.
15. British Library (hereafter BL), Add MS 22285, fo. 60v; Anne Dillon, *The Construction of Martyrdom in the English Catholic Community 1535-1603* (Oxford: Oxford University Press, 2003).
16. T.F. Knox, ed., *Records of the English Catholics under the Penal Laws* Vol. 1 (London: David Nutt, 1878), 360-2.
17. Exeter University Library (hereafter EUL) MS. 95, Canon John Rory Fletcher's mss. Vol. 18, 87-103; John Rory Fletcher, *The Story of the English Bridgettines* (South Brent, Devon: Syon Abbey, 1933), 37-39.
18. Peter Guilday, *The English Catholic Refugees on the Continent 1558-1795* (London: Longman, 1914), xv.
19. F. Donnet, "Les Brigittines Anglaises à Mishagen," *Annales du Congrès Historique et Archéologique de Malines* 2 (1911): 57-58; Guilday, *English Catholic Refugees*, 56.
20. A. De Vlaminck, ed. *L'église collégiale Notre-Dame à Termonde et son ancien obituaire*. Part I (Cercle Archéologique de la ville et de l'ancien pays de Termonde. Publications extraordinaires, VIII Dendermonde, 1898), 280-1.
21. Donnet, "Les Brigittines Anglaises," 56-8.
22. Aungier, *Syon*, 97-8.
23. J. Morris, ed., *Troubles of our Catholic Forefathers* (London: Burns and Oates, 1872-77), Vol. 1, 32-3; Guilday, *English Catholic Refugees*, 378.
24 BL, Add MS 22285, fo. 63 v.
25. David Loades, "Suárez de Figueroa" in *DNB* http://www.oxforddnb.com/view/article/70578 (accessed August 30, 2010); Henry Clifford, *The Life of Jane Dormer, Duchess of Feria*, trans. E.E. Escourt, ed. J. Stevenson (London: Burns and Oates, 1887); Guilday, *English Catholic Refugees,* 4, 43, 57, 201.

26. M.J. Rodriguez-Salgado "Suárez de Figueroa, née Dormer," in *DNB* http://www.oxforddnb.com/view/article/7836 (accessed August 30, 2010).
27. BL, Add MS 22285, fos. 26 v., 191 v.
28. V. Bainbridge, "Newdigate, Sebastian," in *DNB* http://www.oxforddnb.com/view/article/68241 (accessed August 30, 2010); *Calendar of Letters and Papers, Foreign and Domestic, of the Reign of Henry VIII,* Vol.7, 354.
29. W.T. MacCaffrey, "Sidney, Sir Henry," in *DNB* http://www.oxforddnb.com/view/article/255220 (accessed August 30, 2010); H.R. Woudhuysen, "Sidney, Sir Philip," in *DNB* http://www.oxforddnb.com/view/article/25522 (accessed August 30, 2010); Francis R. Johnston, *Syon Abbey* (Eccles: Eccles and District History Society, 1964) 13.
30. Clifford, *Life of Jane Dormer*, 115; Rodriguez-Salgado "Suárez de Figueroa, née Dormer," in *DNB*.
31. G. E. Cokayne et al, *The Complete Peerage,* 12 vols. (London: 2nd. edition, St Catherine Press, 1910-59) Vol. 4, 412; Aungier, *Syon*, 99-100; Michael Questier, *Catholicism and Community in Early Modern England* (Cambridge: Cambridge University Press, 2006).
32. Maurice Chauncy, *Historia Aliquot Martyrum Anglorum* (London: Burns and Oates, 1888), xix-xxv; Geoffrey Anstruther, *A Hundred Homeless Years: English Dominicans 1558-1658* (London: Blackfriars, 1958), 1-15; Guilday, *English Catholic Refugees*, 41-55. The Carthusians were living in a similar situation in Bruges.
33. Guilday, *English Catholic Refugees*, 43, 47, 57.
34. Guilday, *English Catholic Refugees*, 57.
35. Guilday, *English Catholic Refugees*, 58; Donnet, "Les Brigittines Anglaises," 55.
36. T.F. Mayer, "Sander, Nicholas," in *DNB* http://www.oxforddnb.com/view/article/24621 (accessed August 30, 2010); Donnet, "Les Brigittines Anglaises," 58-29.
37. Donnet, "Les Brigittines Anglaises," 56, 60, 62-63. Their interest in the property was eventually sold in 1580; Guildhay, *English Catholic Refugees*, 58.
38. R. Lechat, "Une communauté Anglaise réfugiée à Malines au XVIe Siècle: Les Brigittines de Sion," *Annales du Congrès historique et Archéologique Malines*, 2 (1911): 243-259.
39. Lechat, "Une Communauté Anglaise," 246-49.
40. A.J. Loomie, "Engelfield, Sir Francis," in *DNB* http://oxforddnb.com/view/article/8811 (accessed August 30, 2010).
41. Lechat, "Une Communauté Anglaise," 247.
42. EUL, MS 95, Vol. 12, 138-43, Vol. 19, 35.
43. Lechat, "Une Communauté Anglaise," 253-56.
44. EUL, MS 95 Vol. 19, 73 ; Lechat, "Une Communauté Anglaise," 256-57.
45. Lechat, "Une Communauté Anglaise," 257-58; Guilday, *English Catholic Refugees*, 58.

46. Virginia R. Bainbridge, "Who were the English Bridgettines? The Brothers and Sisters of Syon Abbey, 1415-1600," in *Saint Birgitta, Syon and Vadstena*, eds. Claes Gejrot, Sara Risburg and Mia Äkestam (Stockholm: Kungl. Vitterhets Historie och Antikvitets Akademien, 2010) 37-49; Anstruther, *A Hundred Homeless Years*, 6-14.
47. Knox, *Records of the English Catholics*, 36-2., Aungier, *Syon*, 109.
48. J. Gee, *New Shreds of the Old Snare, containing the apparitions of two new female ghosts etc.* (London: printed by John Dawson for Robert Milbourne, 2nd. edition 1624).
49. Richard Challoner, *Memoirs of Missionary Priests, 1577-1684* (London: Burns and Oates, 1924), 198-202; Morris, *Troubles*, Vol. 1, 138 n; Morris, *Troubles*, Vol. 2, 127-30; Pamela Y. Stanton, "Arundel Family," in *DNB* http://www.oxforddnb.com/view/article/41331 (accessed August 30, 2010).
50. Cokayne, *Complete Peerage*, Vol.12, Part 1, 308-309; Peter Marshall, *Beliefs and the Dead in Reformation England* (Oxford: University of Oxford Press, 2002), 242-45.
51. Kate Aughterson, "Arundell, Dorothy," in *DNB* http://www.oxforddnb.com/view/article/68019 (accessed August 30, 2010).
52. BL MS 18650; Ann M. Hutchison, ed. "Mary Champney: a Bridgettine Nun under the Rule of Queen Elizabeth I," *Birgittiana* 13 (2002); see also Ann M. Hutchinson, "Syon Abbey: Dissolution, No Decline," *Birgittiana* 2 (1996): 245-59; Ann M. Hutchinson, "Beyond the Margins: the Recusant Bridgettines," in *Studies in St Birgitta and the Brigittine Order* ed. J. Hogg (Salzburg: Analecta Cartusiana, 1993) 267-84.
53. Morris, *Troubles*, Vol. 1, 222-4.
54. Clifford, *Life of Jane Dormer*, 148.
55. Aungier, *Syon,* 99-100.
56. Virginia R. Bainbridge, "Women and Learning in Syon Abbey c.1415-1600," in *Syon Abbey and its Books, 1400-1700* , eds. Edward A. Jones and Alexandra M. Walsham (Woodbridge, Suffolk: Boydell and Brewer, 2010), 82-103.
57. Donnet, "Les Brigittines Anglaises," 61-63; Guilday, *English Catholic Refugees*, 58-59.
58. Guilday, *English Catholic Refugees*, 58-9; Aungier, *Syon*, 108-9.
59. Fletcher, *English Bridgettines*, 70-111.
60. For a summary of the various versions and publication dates see Hutchison, "Beyond the Margins," 269 n.
61. Hamilton, *Angel of Syon*, 82-3, 97-113.
62. Hutchison, "Beyond the Margins," 269 n.
63. I cite the version of *A History of Syon's Wanderings* annotated by J.R. Fletcher, EUL, MS 95, Vol. 19.
64. M. Forster, "Forster, Sir Richard," in *DNB* http://www.oxforddnb.com/index/101075054 (accessed August 30, 2010).
65. EUL, MS 95, Vol. 19, 25-27.
66. EUL, MS 95, Vol.18, 120-23; Knox, *Records of the English Catholics,* 360-2; Fletcher, *English Bridgettines*, 76, dates the document.

67. Bainbridge, "Who were the English Bridgettines?" 48.
68. EUL, MS 95, Vol. 12, 58-60, Vol. 19, 180; David Knowles, *The Religious Orders in England* Vol. 3(Cambridge: University of Cambridge Press, 1959) 238; A. Davidson, "Roman Catholicism in Oxforshire, c.1580-1640" (PhD diss., University of Bristol, 1970), 178, 256-59; Hutchison, "Beyond the Margins," 281.
69. Morris, *Troubles*, Vol. 2, 268; BL, MS 22285, fo. 2 r.
70. EUL, MS 95, Vol. 19, 210-15.
71. EUL, MS 95, Vol. 19, 43, 45.
72. EUL, MS 95, Vol. 19, 48.
73. EUL, MS 95, Vol. 19, 69-71.
74. EUL, MS 95, Vol. 19, 73-5.
75. EUL, MS 95, Vol. 19, 73.
76. EUL, MS 95, Vol. 19, 59.
77. EUL, MS 95, Vol. 19, 141.
78. EUL, MS 95, Vol. 19, 127.
79. Fletcher, *English Bridgettines*, 107 n.
80. EUL, MS 95, Vol. 19, 139, 141.
81. EUL MS 95, Vol. 19, 145.
82. Aungier, *Syon,* 97-99.
83. Questier, *Catholicism and Community*, 8, 332-3, 387-400; Glyn Redworth, *The Prince and the Infanta* (New Haven: University of Yale Press, 2003).
84. C. de Hamel, ed. *Syon Abbey, the Library of the Bridgettine Nuns and their Peregrinations after the Reformation* (London: Roxburgh Club, 1991).
85. Thomas Robinson, *The Anatomy of the English Nunnery at Lisbon* (London, 1622).
86. Glyn Redworth, *The She-Apostle* (Oxford: University of Oxford Press, 2008), 81, 205-6.
87. Questier, *Catholicism and Community*, 8, 417-25, 482-86; Forster, "Forster, Sir Richard," in *DNB*.
88. Claire Walker, *Gender and Politics in Early Modern Europe: English Convents in France and the Low Countries* (Basingstoke: Palgrave, 2003); Walker, "Continuity and Isolation.'"
89. Walsham, "Miracles and the Counter-Reformation Mission to England," 786-94.
90. *The Bible*, Psalm 137.
91. EUL, Syon Abbey unnumbered MS: "English Saintes of Kinges and Bishoppes in the primitive times of the Catholique church;" Michael E. Williams, "Paintings of Early British Kings and Queens at Syon Abbey, Lisbon," *Birgittiana* 1 (1996): 123-34.

CHAPTER THREE

"AN UNQUIET ESTATE ABROAD": THE RELIGIOUS EXILE OF CATHOLIC NOBLEWOMEN AND GENTLEWOMEN UNDER ELIZABETH I

KATY GIBBONS

Amongst the wealth of observations in his *Reformation: Europe's House Divided*, Diarmaid MacCulloch notes that the role of women in religious exile has been largely overlooked. In the case of Protestants who left England in the reign of Mary, MacCulloch argues that those devoted and wealthy women who were the backbone of the Protestant movement overseas were until recently "virtually written out of the story of the Marian exile."[1] In recent years, the study of Tudor exiles has become an area of growing interest, but one in which gender issues are rarely fully explored.[2] With the notable exception of female religious, women's role in Catholic exile is perhaps even more neglected than their Protestant counterparts.

This chapter seeks to demonstrate that by including women in our account of Catholic exile under Elizabeth I, we can not only expand our understanding of exile and its political meanings, but also revisit arguments about the role of women in the English Catholic community. A number of highborn English Catholic laywomen did not remain at home when their husbands and fathers went into exile in the later sixteenth century. This chapter explores the experience of three women: Anne Percy, Countess of Northumberland; Elizabeth Johnson; and Katherine Copley. Their departure from England can be explained initially by the actions of their male relatives, but their responses to dislocation and dispossession were complex. Their removal overseas provoked practical problems, but their flight, and the privileged status they might claim as highborn women suffering for their faith, also offered new opportunities.

There were some elements of exile in which women can be seen to be particularly significant: their contribution to the financial status of their family whilst abroad; their role as an example both to their coreligionists and their children; and the extent to which their actions strengthened family strategy. This chapter argues that the problems and dilemmas of religious exile, and female responses to them in the sixteenth century, deserve further consideration. They reveal a more complex picture of the exile experience, whilst also suggesting how women played a "public" part in the internationalisation of the English Catholic cause in the early modern period.

The historiography of religious exile

The central role occupied by women in post-Reformation Catholicism in England has long been recognised.[3] Traditionally, this was seen to fit a narrative in which gentle and noble Catholicism retreated from public life. In the face of government persecution, Catholics increasingly withdrew into private households, rendering crucial the role of the wife, mother or sister as household manager. The centrality of the matriarch was recognised by contemporary commentators who praised individuals such as Dorothy Lawson and Lady Montague.[4] Historians have subsequently expanded this theme, considering for example the challenge that their behaviour presented to the Protestant regime. John Bossy stressed that the Catholicism of such women was "active and proselytising rather than merely domestic," a point recently reinforced by Clare Walker.[5] To withdraw from parish worship and pursue Catholic devotions had increasingly political implications; Catholic women were thus issuing a challenge to the Protestant Crown. Recent trends in women's and gender history have challenged the assumed dichotomy between public and private spheres in the early modern world.[6] This complicates the traditional assumption that women operated as Catholics within their family estates whilst their husbands engaged with the wider world. Catholic gentlewomen could also act outside the "normal" context of the household by exploiting a number of opportunities, albeit contested. Those women who went into exile in particular took up roles which had clear "public" consequences. Their activity abroad was significant not only for their families, but for the wider Catholic community, and for Protestant authorities at home.

Recent decades have seen increasing interest in the links between Catholics in England and those on the continent, including Catholic exile in the sixteenth and seventeenth centuries.[7] Burgeoning research on the

English Catholic convents established on the continent from the end of the seventeenth century will expand our understanding of a particularly prominent form of English Catholic exile; but detailed exploration of laywomen who went overseas before the foundation of the convents is rather lacking.[8] This can partly be explained by the fragmented nature of surviving source material: laywomen who moved around are difficult to track. The official documentation of the Protestant government, concerned with undermining the political activities of conspirators, focuses on exceptional individuals rather than everyday experience; only incidental mention is made of wives and children who accompanied male exiles. The notable exceptions were those women directly involved in anti-government activity abroad. Other women, leaving little written record of their experiences, can only be approached through the filter of male kin or hostile government agents.

The contemporary context for female exiles

The status of Catholics who left Protestant England and the meanings of their departures were highly contested by contemporaries. Catholics abroad styled themselves as exiles banished for their religion, or as peaceable men and women in search of freedom of conscience. To the Protestant government, they were fugitives and potential traitors, posing a direct political threat to the state. There were in fact several different forms of Catholic residence abroad.[9] For the purposes of this chapter, however, Catholics overseas will be referred to as exiles: although a volatile category, it was one with which contemporaries were familiar.

The treatment of female members of the Catholic community raised a number of legal questions, and became the focus of discussion in often heated Parliamentary debates over anti-Catholic legislation. The position of the wives of Catholic offenders, or indeed Catholic wives whose husbands had not offended, was contested.[10] More pertinent, however, were debates about the treatment of Catholic couples who went into exile collectively or separately. From 1571, a raft of legislation explicitly associated withdrawal from England with the service of foreign princes and collusion with rebels.[11] Those leaving unlicensed, or exceeding the limits of their licence, were to lose lands and property unless returning and submitting to the Crown. Women featured in Parliamentary discussions concerning the banishment of religious non-conformists. By the early 1590s, the government had experimented briefly with banishment as a means of dealing with Catholic priests, and with laity who were repeatedly prosecuted for non-attendance at the state church. The question was whether banishment should apply to the spouse and children of individuals. If a wife did not accompany the banished man, the financial burden of maintaining them at home would have to be met.[12] These were by no means abstract debates: the presence in England of the wives and children of exiles was a present reality. Christopher Danby, a rebel against the Crown in 1569, fled to the continent with his fellow rebels. In his absence, Christopher's wife Margaret apparently relied on her brother-in-law Sir Thomas Danby for financial support.[13] Evidently, the Danbys were not an isolated case.

Women in Exile: Three Case Studies

Anne Percy, Countess of Northumberland

Perhaps the most prominent female exile was Anne Percy, Countess of Northumberland, wife of the seventh Earl. Anne's father, Henry Somerset, Earl of Worcester, was a Catholic sympathiser, but unlike his daughter made no open commitment to an oppositional stance. Anne's approach had clear political consequences. Her exile was directly provoked by participation in the rebellion of 1569, an uprising against the Protestant Crown in the north of England. Anne's husband, Thomas Percy, Earl of Northumberland was one of its leaders; and, even bearing in mind the hostile nature of the evidence, Anne herself was also significant in the rising. Government agents reported that in the run up to the revolt, the Earl was close to seeking mercy from the Crown. However, Anne, "beyng the stowter of the two, dothe hasten hym and yncourage hym to persever." Although heavily pregnant, she rode "up and down with... [the rebels'] army from place to place."[14]

Anne was the only woman named by the Crown as an instigator of the revolt in her own right, and the Queen allegedly declared that she "behoved to be burnt, and merited it well."[15] Although some Catholic writers may have sought to refute this, the association of Anne Percy with the revolt was one that stuck.[16] Protestant polemic alleged the moral and sexual corruption of the rebels' wives. One 1569 publication claimed the wives had persuaded their husbands to restore Catholicism by force only because they wanted to satisfy their carnal lusts with Catholic priests: "few women storme against the marriage of Priestes, calling it unlawfull, and incensing men against it, but such as have bene Priestes harlots or fayne woulde be."[17]

However exaggerated or distorted these reports, Anne's activism during and after the revolt is evident. The Earl was imprisoned in Scotland, but Anne escaped to the Spanish Low Countries. From a position of apparent poverty, she spent the following months working for her husband's liberation, corresponding with Catholic leaders on the continent to raise money for his ransom.[18] Anne made preparations for the Earl to join her, and wrote to him of her activity, encouraging him to keep his spirits up. In January 1571, for instance, she assured him that despite considerable difficulty, funds from the Pope and Philip II were apparently forthcoming. She gave her husband instructions to organise and conduct his journey to Europe. Clearly Anne was more than capable of independent action. Having negotiated with Catholic powers in Europe on her husband's behalf, she was in a good position to offer him advice. However, her correspondence was couched in a discourse of inferiority: "For mine own parte, being but a Woman, I can no more pray for your good successe and spede, seing the matter is to weightie for me to give Advice upon, and to chargeable to intermeddle with."[19] This was perhaps intended as a means for her husband to save face: clearly she had "intermeddled" in such matters. In the end, neither her claims to inferiority nor her political appeals succeeded in obtaining her husband's release and relocation. The Earl fell into English hands and was executed for treason in 1572.

Although a married woman, Anne was in exile without her husband and perhaps with only one child. Her correspondence revealed she was keen for their move abroad, feeling that their eldest daughter in particular would benefit: "her Age is fittest to receave Instruction, and most readie to take knowledge now of the virtuous examples whiche here she should see and learne."[20] However, she was anxious for the discretion and safety of their journey: she felt that they might follow separately at a later date. She possibly took with her the infant Mary, born during her stay in Scotland, but ultimately her other daughters remained in England.[21] In some respects, however, the absence of husband and children may have conferred a particular status and freedom of manoeuvre abroad. After his execution, the earl was presented by Catholic propagandists as a martyr, and Anne herself can be seen as playing some role in this process. Taking on the mantle of the aristocratic widow, who like the Earl had suffered for her faith, Anne remained dedicated to defending her husband's name. Although the evidence is hazy, she is generally thought to have had a hand in a French tract, *Discours des troubles nouellement aduenuz en Angleterre au moys d'octobre 1569* (1570), which closes with a French translation of the declaration made by the Earls in 1569.[22] Intriguingly, the work is fairly mild in tone, lacking the vitriol of hostile Protestant polemic on the revolt. Nonetheless, Daniella Busse has recently argued that the 1570 work was actually written to rally support for the revolt on the continent.[23] Elizabeth's minister William Cecil apparently recognised this, and saw fit to write a rejoinder, the manuscript of which survives.[24] A biographer of the seventh Earl claims that Anne later wrote a rebuke to Cecil, which was published in France. He attributes to the countess a work entitled *Discours des Troubles du Conte de Northumberland*, published in Liège in 1572, which apparently championed her husband as a loyal nobleman who had been the victim of persecution. Unfortunately, the survival of this work is unclear.[25] In any case, the Countess was associated with polemic directed at an international audience relating to the revolt, and the status of her husband as a martyr for the English Catholic cause grew in the course of her lifetime.[26]

Anne Percy's existence on the continent was more precarious than her previous life in England. The earldom was passed to her brother-in-law, Henry Percy, and in theory her rebellion and flight destroyed any hope of receiving revenues from home. On the continent, she also faced a number of challenges. The government's demands for the expulsion or extradition of fugitive Catholics from Habsburg territories, together with the revolt of the Netherlands against Spanish Catholic rule, combined to make a certain existence unlikely for English Catholics abroad.[27] The Countess had to cope with being expelled from Habsburg lands thanks to Anglo-Spanish diplomacy, and had her belongings sacked by troops in 1572. Although she considered moving to Italy, she remained in the Low Countries region. During her twenty-year exile she was recorded at Bruges, Mechlin, Antwerp, Brussels, Liège and Namur.[28] This movement appears not to have curtailed her opposition to the Elizabethan government. The Countess' efforts to defend her husband's name can be seen as part of a wider undertaking to rally support for the cause of English Catholicism on a European stage. Her household became a centre for exiles in search of contacts and support. The Countess received a large pension from the Spanish King, given on the grounds that it would support her and others in her charge.[29] She employed men to cross the Channel and keep her informed of events at home, whilst involving herself with continental projects relating to the future of England. She corresponded with the Spanish authorities in support of a Catholic invasion, and was involved in plans for the liberation of the imprisoned Mary Stuart, the deposed Queen of Scotland and heir to the English throne.[30] Although this activity did not result in the restoration of Catholicism, Elizabeth I was right to single Anne out as someone to be watched carefully.[31]

After over twenty years in exile, Anne Percy died in a convent in Namur, possibly of smallpox. By this point, she had acquired some personal wealth, but her exile appears to have taken its toll.[32] Both Catholic and Protestant sources reported that she had been driven mad by the difficulties of her exile.[33] The impact of Anne's exile on her children deserves further scrutiny: whilst it was not unusual for the offspring of noble families to spend time apart from their parents, Anne's absence was more enforced than usual. At least three of her daughters grew up in England and were married there, forging connections with other Catholic families.[34] Mary was an infant when her mother fled, and her mother possibly took her with her in 1570, although the details of her subsequent childhood are similarly unclear.[35] However, we do know that Mary went on to commit to an exile of her own from the late 1590s. She entered religious life as a founding member, and later abbess, of the English Benedictine house at Brussels.[36]

One of the reasons for Anne's appearance in extant source material is the unusual nature of her position abroad. An activist and the widow of a martyr, Anne became something of a figurehead for her fellow exiles. The separation from her children for at least part of her exile changed the tone of her exile, whilst also increasing her ability to act without the conventional ties of a highborn Catholic woman inside England. Anne's activism provoked attention from fellow exiles, foreign Catholic powers, and the English government. The unsettled situation in the Low Countries presented immediate practical problems, but also offered a new stage for action.

Elizabeth Johnson

The second case study bears both similarities and differences to Anne Percy. Elizabeth Johnson, born Elizabeth Norton, came from a prosperous and well-established gentry family in the North Riding of Yorkshire. Elizabeth's exile also sprang from connections to the 1569 revolt. The Nortons were known for their activism in defence of their faith. Her father Richard was a key gentry ringleader; her uncle and brother were executed in the aftermath. Richard fled first to Scotland, then to the Low Countries in 1572, accompanied by several of his sons, and presumably also Elizabeth. Unlike Anne Percy, detailed information about her life overseas is lacking. She joined her male relatives abroad for at least some of their exile. Initially in an impoverished state, they spent time in the Low Countries, Rome and Northern France, and were involved in agitation for action against the Protestant regime in England.[37]

Judging from the available evidence, Elizabeth was not a passive observer of the activity of her male relatives. Her husband Henry Johnson was attainted for his part in the revolt, and his execution was expected. However, partly on the grounds that he was "very simple," and had been "abused by his wife" into taking part, Henry was pardoned in 1573.[38] The suggestion of Elizabeth's personal responsibility probably combined with the fact that Johnson's lands had already been made over to her, so the Crown would not gain financially by his execution.[39] Nevertheless, it is perhaps not surprising that Elizabeth, like Anne Percy, was cast as a dominating wife and blamed for her husband's rebellion, and her flight overseas served as a useful measure of disobedience. If there is any sense in which Henry was led by his wife, her influence was not curtailed by a move abroad. Interestingly, both Elizabeth and her husband feature in subsequent government reports on those considered to be acting subversively abroad: it appears that Henry may have had a pension from Rome, and in 1580 their children may have been in Paris.[40] In fact, Elizabeth may even have returned to England: various accounts suggest her imprisonment for religion in the late 1570s and 1580s.[41]

Elizabeth's precise movements overseas are, unfortunately, unclear. The first statement from Elizabeth herself dates from 1585, when she was appealing for permission to resettle in England. By this point, she was in Scotland, and had approached the English ambassador there to advance her case. Her petition and the ambassador's accompanying letter of intercession both survive. Elizabeth was at pains to deny the political or religious nature of her exile. She claimed to have left England out of duty to her father, acting as his companion and nurse: "Nature moved me his daughter not to leave him in his old age."[42] She stressed her desire to "quietly repair without molestation into my native country, ther to submit my self to her Majesties will and pleasure to the end that I may spend the rest of my lyfe lyke a trew Subject."[43]

Much of Elizabeth's appeal can be understood as a recognised rhetoric of petition, employed to maximise the chances of success. Contemporary petitions often emphasised a lack of personal agency: Elizabeth stressed her role as her father's nurse and her lack of choice in leaving England. Such an approach was determined by the inferiority of the petitioner's status, and the expectation that a submissive attitude was more likely to get results.[44] Like other female petitioners who claimed family responsibilities as mitigating circumstances, Elizabeth presented her unlicensed departure as a consequence of her female status.[45]

Significantly, the timing of Elizabeth's petition for pardon was shaped by her male relatives. Elizabeth's brother George had decided to end his exile existence. He provided intelligence on conspiratorial circles abroad – in which he and his father were involved – in order to gain a return home.[46] In fact, George's pardon, backed by key members of Elizabeth's regime, was being obtained when Elizabeth appealed for similar treatment. Presumably she hoped her brother's contacts might help her case.[47] She could not offer the Crown intelligence, but she could adopt a persona unavailable to George: the submissive daughter, who had left only to care for her father.

Any account of Elizabeth's personal motivations for abjuring her exile status can only be speculative. Her intercessor with the English Crown claimed that she realised "the difference betwene a dutifull and quiet lyf at home, and an unquiet estate abroad."[48] Perhaps this contained some genuine sentiment, but the position of her father here seems instrumental. Elizabeth crossed the Channel with Richard in 1585, at which point there are contradictory accounts of his position. Some suggested he was en route for an English prison, whilst contemporary Catholic accounts say he was heading for Scotland.[49] In any case, Richard was dying: he made a will on board ship, in which his daughter was named executrix. Any funds belonging to him in his places of exile were assigned to Elizabeth. She had a specific role assigned her by her father, who had "committed certaine speciall matters" to her charge.[50]

Quite what these responsibilities were remains unknown, but the suggestion is that, having been a central member of the family in exile, she was given a key role in safeguarding the little remaining wealth of the Nortons. The sources are unfortunately silent about Elizabeth's subsequent position. Unlike her brother, Elizabeth does not appear on the Patent Rolls as a recipient of the Queen's pardon, although this itself is not proof that she was unsuccessful.[51] It is possible that she re-entered England permanently without a pardon; it was not uncommon for Catholics who had gone abroad unlicensed to return to England and escape government reprisals.

Whilst the cause of Elizabeth's exile was comparable to that of Anne Percy, their paths diverged in terms of practical experience and resolution. Unlike the widowed Countess, she lacked the status, resources and opportunity for an independent existence. Elizabeth's exile career was shaped by the position of her father, brothers and husband. Her exile, which acted to confirm the notion of Elizabeth as disobedient citizen and domineering wife, helped to ensure the survival of her husband, and the continuance of her family's activities.

Katherine Copley

In contrast, Katherine Copley perhaps presents a more conventional model of the wife in exile, although her story can only be accessed through her husband's correspondence. Sir Thomas Copley was a wealthy and well-connected gentleman. He resisted pressure for a high status marriage in order to marry Katherine Lutterall, from a less illustrious family. A Protestant with close ties to Catholic gentry, Thomas converted at some point in the early 1560s. His conversion was publicly attributed to his discovery of errors in Protestant controversy, but Katherine's Catholicism was presumably also significant.[52] Thomas departed for the continent in 1570, placing his fortune in trust to defend it from government reprisals. This theoretically provided some security for his wife and children, who were to remain in England. However, with a changing legal and political landscape in England, the Crown seized revenues from Copley's lands.[53] Katherine and the children then joined Thomas abroad, where at various points different family members were in the Low Countries, France and Spain.[54]

The family suffered mixed fortunes abroad. Some exiles looked to Thomas for moral support and advice, whilst the government suspected him of sedition. Throughout his exile, Thomas wrote to Elizabeth's ministers Cecil and Walsingham, also his kinsmen, proclaiming his loyalty. He sought reconciliation with the Crown, whilst defending his acceptance of Spanish and French support. One recurring theme was his family's financial shortage. Copley pleaded that profits from his English estates be allowed to reach them: this would free them from reliance on foreign aid.[55] As it was, their only income from England was a small allowance conceded by the Queen, paid to Katherine, and by the mid-1580s this was being reduced.[56]

Katherine meanwhile presumably set herself to looking after a sizeable family in straightened circumstances.[57] The couple spent periods of time apart, which may not have differed much from their previous existence in England, where gentry couples often lived in separate places for parts of the year. When he was planning a trip to Spain, Thomas told Burghley that correspondence could be sent through Katherine, who was to remain in Paris: "my wife shall still keep her howse, whither soever I be driven by necessitie to goe."[58] Katherine also took on the role of intercessor. In 1574, for instance, the Crown conceded that Katherine could visit England, presumably to deal with family finances; she then rejoined her family in Antwerp. Copley declared in his correspondence that whilst in England she would act as his intercessor, seeking pardon from the Crown.[59] It is not clear whether Katherine openly embraced this role during her visit - a familiar female role to contemporaries - but her husband evidently trusted her abilities in this regard. It seems too that her position as representative of her exiled husband was tacitly accepted by the Crown.

The Copleys' fortunes changed abruptly in 1584, shortly before Thomas' death. Elizabeth I cancelled Katherine's income and demanded her return. The Copleys conceded and Katherine went home. Doing so actually allowed her to maintain the family's connection with Catholicism. She ensured, for example, that her husband's will, which had been drawn up on the continent, was registered and executed in England. Far from being a statement of submission to the Protestant authorities, the will contained clear indications of Thomas' Catholicism.[60] He entrusted to Katherine, his "entirely beloved wife," the care and education of their large family on condition that she not remarry: if she were to do so the responsibility would pass to his Catholic kinsman.[61] Like Elizabeth Johnson, Katherine Copley was entrusted with the care of the family's financial and religious standing. After her husband's death, Katherine did not settle down to a quiet life. She was more openly involved in circles considered dangerous by the government. She was imprisoned for housing Jesuits in 1586, and her subsequent return overseas with some of her children sparked suspicion. By 1590, due to her time abroad and contacts with the Jesuits, the Protestant authorities saw her as a useful source of information. One agent's disparaging assessment of Katherine probably obscures her potential importance: "She is simple enough and unfit to meddle with such things, but as she is a great bigot she will know ther rendezvouz and should be interrogated."[62]

It is unclear how long Katherine stayed overseas. It seems she was still abroad in 1591 at least, when she launched a suit for the restoration of her dower lands in England. Elizabeth Allen reports her as conforming in England by 1596, possibly in an attempt to avoid financial penalties, yet there was serious suspicion about the people she housed, who were suspected of "launching great practices."[63] Whilst Thomas lived, it seemed Katherine was viewed as less of a threat than her husband. The couple established something resembling a "traditional" gentry household, albeit one lived in exile. In some respects Katherine fulfilled the function ascribed to Catholic gentlewoman in England: the maintenance of a household and the perpetuation of Catholicism in the next generation. Katherine's children followed a variety of directions. Her sons were educated in English Catholic institutions on the continent: one became a Catholic priest then an Anglican vicar; another returned to England but was later exiled for involvement in Catholic plots. Her daughters had contacts with religious houses on the continent, and some of her granddaughters entered English convents overseas.[64] Katherine's adoption of an expected role, and her apparent distance from activity against the Crown whilst Thomas lived was perhaps a deliberate strategy. Adopting this position during her husband's lifetime possibly ensured the financial support the family received from England, and may have eased her passage into a widowhood more actively engaged in contentious activity.

Conclusion

These women suggest a number of different roles for Catholic women in exile. The prominence of Anne led her to stand out in the eyes of contemporaries, but all her activity did not result in a return to the homeland. Elizabeth Johnson's experience was heavily shaped by that of her male relatives – her father probably more than her husband. Of the three, Katherine Copley seems to most reflect the expected role of a Catholic matriarch, although her continental sojourns complicated this considerably and gave her actions political import. Without downplaying the very real difficulties – practical, personal and ideological – these women confronted, their flight, and the privileged status they might claim as highborn women suffering for their faith, also offered new opportunities.

The roles these women adopted in exile were by no means static: each was in constant negotiation with a number of parties, at home and overseas. Anne Percy, Elizabeth Johnson and Katherine Copley demonstrate the multiple courses of action open to Catholic women abroad, and the possibility of changing their stance over time. Their positions were informed by the Protestant government in England as well as the families and exile communities of which they were a part. Thus a number of factors, including national and regional politics, contingency and personal agency, informed their different stories; but the role of exile was also shaped by the multiple roles of wives, daughters, mothers and sisters, which could demand from them different strategies. These women discussed here by no means exhaust the possibilities for female experiences of exile, but it is hoped that they suggest scope for further study. A consideration of female contributions to Catholicism inside England should be extended to those living in what one hostile contemporary referred to as "an unquiet estate abroad."

Notes

The author thanks audience members at the West of England and South Wales Women's History Network conference, Bristol, 2007 and at the Rethinking Politics Conference, Warwick, 2009, where various aspects of this research was presented; and the anonymous reader for constructive comments.

1. Diarmaid MacCulloch, *Reformation: Europe's House Divided, 1490-1700* (London: Penguin, 2003), 657.
2. Peter Marshall, "Exiles and the Tudor State," in *Discipline and Diversity*, eds. Kate Cooper and Jeremy Gregory (Studies in Church History 43, 2007): 263-284; Peter Marshall, "'The Greatest Man in Wales': James ap Gruffydd ap Hywel and the International Opposition to Henry VIII," *Sixteenth Century Journal*, 39 (2008): 681-704; Alec Ryrie, *The Gospel and Henry VIII: Evangelicals in the early English Reformation* (Cambridge: Cambridge University Press, 2003), ch. 3.
3. John Bossy, *The English Catholic Community, 1570-1880* (London: Darton, Longman and Todd, 1975), 153-60; Marie B. Rowlands, "Harbourers and Housekeepers: Catholic Women in England, 1570-1720," in *Catholic Communities in Protestant States*, eds. Benjamin J. Kaplan, Bob Moore, Henk van Nierop and Judith Pollmann (Manchester: Manchester University Press, 2009), 200-215.
4. Clare Walker, "Dorothy Lawson," in *The Oxford Dictionary of National Biography*, [hereafter ODNB] eds. H. C. G. Matthew and Brian Harrison, 60 vols.. (Oxford: Oxford University Press, 2004), 32: 883-84; Mervyn James, *Family, Lineage and Civil Society: a Study of Society, Politics and Mentality in the Durham Region, 1500-1640* (Oxford: Clarendon Press 1974), 137-42; Michael Questier, *Catholicism and Community in Early Modern England: Politics, Aristocratic Patronage and Religion, c. 1550-1640* (Cambridge: Cambridge University Press, 2006), 209-30.
5. Bossy, *English Catholic Community,* 157; Walker, "Lawson," 883-4.
6. Leonore Davidoff, "Gender and the 'Great Divide': Public and Private in British Gender History," *Journal of Women's History* 15 (2003): 11-27; Amanda Vickery, "Golden Age to Separate Spheres: A Review of the Categories and Chronology of English Women's History," *Historical Journal* 36 (1993): 383-414.
7. John Anthony Bossy, "Elizabethan Catholicism: The Link with France" (PhD diss., University of Cambridge, 1960); Anne Dillon, *The Construction of Martyrdom in the English Catholic Community, 1535-1603* (Aldershot: Ashgate, 2002); Clare Walker, *Gender and Politics in Early Modern Europe: English Convents in France and the Low Countries* (Basingstoke: Palgrave Macmillan, 2003); Katy Gibbons, *The English Catholic Community in Paris* (forthcoming).
8. "Who were the Nuns? " A Prosopographical study of the English Convents in exile 1600-1800; led by Michael Questier at Queen Mary University London. See http://wwtn.history.qmul.ac.uk/.
9. Gibbons, *English Catholics and Exile*, ch. 4.

10. Bossy, *English Catholic Community*, 153-55; Marie B. Rowlands, "Recusant Women 1560-1640," in *Women in English Society 1500-1800*, ed. Mary Prior (London: Routledge, 1985),153-54.
11. *The Statutes of the Realm,* 11 vols.. (London: Dawsons, 1963), 3: part 1, 531-34.
12. K. J. Kesselring, *Mercy and Authority in the Tudor State* (Cambridge: Cambridge University Press, 2003), 32-35. For debates in Parliament, J. E. Neale, *Elizabeth I and her Parliaments 1584-1601* (London: Cape, 1957), 280-97.
13. North Yorkshire County Record Office, Northallerton, ZS Swinton Estate and Middleham Estate Records, (Microfilm, Reel 2087, Item 000422), Margaret Danby to Thomas Danby, Beeston, April 2 1587; Krista Kesselring, *The Northern Rebellion of 1569: Faith, Politics and Protest in Elizabethan England* (Basingstoke: Palgrave Macmillan, 2007), 139.
14. Cuthbert Sharp, *Memorials of the Rebellion of 1569* (London: J. B. Nichols and Son, 1840), 77. For the revolt, Susan E. Taylor, "The Crown and the North of England, 1559-70: A Study of the Rebellion of the Northern Earls 1569-70 and its Causes " (PhD diss., University of Manchester, 1981); Kesselring, *Rebellion.*
15. Kesselring, *Rebellion*, 138; Anne Somerset, *Elizabeth I* (London: St Martins Press, 1992), 301.
16. Daniella Busse, "Anti-Catholic Polemical Writing on the 'Rising in the North' (1569) and the Catholic Reaction," *Recusant History* 27 (2004): 20.
17. Thomas Norton, *To the Quenes Maiesties poore deceived subiects of the northe contreye* (1569): D 2 v. Cited in K. J. Kesselring, "'A Cold Pye for the Papistes': Constructing and Containing the Northern Rising of 1569," *Journal of British Studies* 43 (2004): 438. A generation previously, Protestant women were accused by Catholic polemicists of sexual licence. Thomas Freeman, "'The Good Ministrie of Godly and Virtuouse Women': The Elizabethan Martyrologists and the Female Supporters of Marian Martyrs," *Journal of British Studies* 39 (2000): 25.
18. Sharp, *Memorials*, 346; Julian Lock, "Thomas Percy" in *ODNB*, 15:744; Robert Lechat, *Les Réfugiés Anglais dans les Pays-Bays Espagnols durant le règne d'Élisabeth 1558-1603* (Louvain: Bureau de Recueils, 1914), 44.
19. William Murdin, ed. *A Collection of State Papers Relating to Affairs in the Reign of Queen Elizabeth* (London: William Bowyer, 1759), 189.
20. Murdin, *Collection*, 191.
21. Sharp, *Memorials*, 350; Philip Caraman, *The Other Face: Catholic Life under Elizabeth I* (London: Longmans, 1960); Lock, "Thomas Percy," 745.
22 *Discours des troubles nouellement aduenuz en Angleterre au moys d'octobre 1569* (Lyon, 1570). Another work published in 1570 by the same printer reported the revolt but was anti-English in tone: *Continuation des choses plus célèbres & mémorables advenues en Angleterre, Escosse et Irlande* (Lyon, 1570). For English Protestant polemic, Busse, "Anti-Catholic"; Kesselring, "'A Cold Pye'" and *Rebellion*; James K. Lowers, *Mirrors for Rebels: a study of Polemical Literature Relating to the Northern Rebellion, 1569* (Berkeley: University of California Press, 1953).
23. Busse, "Anti-Catholic,"25.

24. The National Archives, London [hereafter TNA] SP 12/66/55.
25. M. M. Merrick, *Thomas Percy, Seventh Earl* (London: Duckett, 1949), 123. The only work recorded by the St Andrews French Vernacular Book project is *Discours*, cited in n. 22. There were two editions in 1570, and five in 1587. *French Vernacular Books*: *Books Published in the French language before 1601*, eds. Andrew Pettegree et al, 2 vols.. (Leiden: Brill, 2007), 2:538-9, nos 42820-42827. Those editions I have consulted are not markedly radical.
26. Kesselring, *Rebellion*, 171-178.
27. Lechat, *Réfugiés*; J. J. E. Proost, "Les Réfugiés Anglais et Irlandais en Belgique, à la suite de la Réforme religieuse établie sous Élizabeth et Jacques Ier," *Messager des Sciences Historiques* (1865): 277-314.
28. Sharp, *Memorials*, 346-50; Merrick, *Percy*, 124; Lock, "Thomas Percy," 744-45.
29. A. J. Loomie, *The Spanish Elizabethans: the English Exiles at the Court of Philip II* (London: Burns and Oates, 1963), 95; *The First and the Second Diaries of the English College, Douay*, ed. Thomas Francis Knox (London: D. Nutt, 1969), 298-301; Lechat, *Réfugiés*, 140-41, 234; Murdin, *Collection*, 49; Sharp, *Memorials*, 348.
30. Sharp, *Memorials*, 347-48.
31. Somerset, *Elizabeth*, 301; Lechat, *Réfugiés*, 123.
32. Sharp, *Memorials*, 348; TNA, SP 12/240/19, Charles Paget to Thomas Barnes, September 23/October 3 1591.
33. Sidney Lee, "Thomas Percy," in *Dictionary of National Biography*, eds. Leslie Stephen and Sidney Lee, 22 vols.. (London: Oxford University Press, 1885-1900), 15:880; Lock, "Thomas Percy," 745.
34. Sharp, *Memorials*, 350.
35. Lock argues that the Countess took her youngest daughter with her: Lock, "Thomas Percy," 745; others suggest that all her children were left behind: Sharp, *Memorials*, 350.
36. Caroline M. K. Bowden, "Lady Mary Percy," in *ODNB*, 43:734.
37. Gibbons, *The English Catholic Community in Paris,* ch. 4.
38. Taylor, 'Crown', Appendix I, 122.
39. Sharp, *Memorials*, 226.
40. Clare Talbot, ed., "Miscellanea Recusant Records," *Catholic Record Society* [hereafter *CRS*] 53 (1960): 212; TNA, SP 78/48a/279.
41. "Miscellanea I," ed. J. H. Pollen, *CRS*, 1 (1905): 60, 62; "The Douay College Diaries, Third, Fourth and Fifth: 1598-1654," ed. Edwin H. Burton, *CRS*, 11 (1911): 563; Michael Hicks, "Richard Norton," in *ODNB*, 41: 183.
42. TNA, SP 52/37/56, Petition of Elizabeth Johnson to Mr Wootton, [June?] 1585.
43. TNA, SP 52/37/56.
44. Lynne Magnusson, "'A Rhetoric of Requests': Genre and Linguistic Scripts in Elizabethan Women's Suitors' Letters," in *Women and Politics in Early Modern England (1450-1700)*, ed. James Daybell (Aldershot: Ashgate, 2004), 58-64.
45. Kesselring, *Mercy*, 109, 115.

46. Gibbons, *The English Catholic Community in Paris*, ch. 4.
47. TNA, SP 52/37/69, Francis Walsingham to Edward Wootton, 17 June 1585.
48. TNA, SP/52/37/55, Edward Wootton to Francis Walsingham, 7 June 1585.
49. Hicks, "Richard Norton": 183; "Letters of William Allen and Richard Barrett, 1572-1598," ed. P. Renold, *CRS*, 58 (1996): 155.
50. "North Country Wills, Vol. II," Surtees *Society*, 121 (1912): 120. In fact, any property he left as a foreigner in France would have be seized by the French Crown under the *droit d'aubain*.
51. Kesselring, *Mercy*, 73-74, 210-11.
52. Richard Copley Christie, ed., *Letters of Sir Thomas Copley*, (London: Roxburghe Club, 1897), xxiii; Michael A. R. Graves, "Thomas Copley," in *ODNB*, 13: 359.
53. *Copley*, xxvii.
54. *Copley*, Introduction. Their youngest son was sent to England as a newborn baby, but returned to the continent aged 9.
55. TNA, SP 15/27a/94, Thomas Copley to Walsingham, Rouen, 5 July 1582; *Copley*, 162.
56. *Copley*, 162.
57. Graves, "Thomas Copley," 359; and "Anthony Copley," in *ODNB*, 13:342; Elizabeth Allen, "John Copley," in *ODNB*, 13:345.
58. *Copley*, 131.
59. *Copley*, 22.
60. *Copley*, Appendix, 181-91.
61. TNA, PROB 11/68, f. 1-1v.
62. *Calendar of State Papers, Domestic Series in the Reigns of Elizabeth and James I, Addenda*, 1580-1625, ed. Mary Anne Everett Green (London: H.M.S.O., 1872), 311.
63. Allen, "John Copley," 345; *Copley*, xl.
64. Graves, "Anthony Copley," 342-43; Allen, "John Copley," 345; *Copley*, xli-xlviii.

CHAPTER FOUR

FRANCAISE OU AMERICAN?: THE IMMIGRATION STORY OF JOSEPHINE DUPONT, 1795 TO 1833

EVELYN KASSOUF SPRATT

"I should have preferred greatly to remain in France for the time being and to follow our own opportunities of fortune," wrote Josephine du Pont in 1826.[1] Even though she had settled in America twenty-six years earlier and was the wife of a prominent naturalized American, Josephine du Pont's longing for France permeated her correspondence and memoirs. "Dear France," she wrote, "the object of so many thoughts, projects and unfruitful regrets."[2] These sentiments, written always in French because she never became fluent in English, pepper her writings and reveal her continued desire to return home. As an older woman, she still did not feel at home and clung to a French identity within the geographic and cultural borders of America.

This paper is a story of one French woman's immigration to America at the beginning of the nineteenth century. Much current scholarship on immigration considers the reasons people left their homelands, their expectations for life in America and the quantitative demographics of immigrants. Additionally, many studies examine the legal status of immigrants and the development of the naturalization process in the New Republic.[3] How the experiences affected individual men and women and what effects immigration had on their identities and the role it played within their families remain unexamined.

Josephine Pelleport du Pont's various memoirs and correspondence from her life in *ancien régime* France, revolutionary France, and the new republics in France and America provide rich insights into a tumultuous time in French and American history. At first reading, Josephine's memoirs and correspondence seem mundane. However, when these documents are considered together and placed within the political, social and cultural contexts of late eighteenth century America and France, they shed light upon several broader themes such as experiences of early immigrants to America, gender roles in the New Republic, and cultural and national identities. This story of Josephine du Pont seeks to clarify the insights of an elite woman who chose not to assume an American national identity but instead to perpetuate her French cultural identity.

Josephine's life in France and America

Gabrielle Josephine de La Fite de Pelleport was born on March 20, 1770, to an aristocratic French family. Her parents died before the Revolution, and she was cared for by various family members until she married Victor du Pont, eldest son of the famed physiocrat, Pierre Samuel du Pont de Nemours. After their marriage in 1794, Victor accepted a position in the French consulate in Charleston, South Carolina. By 1798 political relations between France and America had deteriorated and the du Ponts returned to France. In 1800, Victor, his younger brother Eluthère Irenée (E.I.), their wives and children and the patriarch of the family, du Pont de Nemours, moved to America with the intent of setting up a business in either land speculation or trade between France and America. Various factors led to the failure of the first du Pont company. Many historians have attributed the lack of success to Victor's inability to manage a business. It is clear, however, that other issues contributed to the problems such as difficult political relations between the United States and France and the location of the company (New York City). The du Pont Company ultimately declared bankruptcy.

In order to survive financially, E.I. sought out land to develop a gun powder business. A trained chemist, he had developed an expertise in this area in France and saw a need for it in America. He found land in Delaware and the entire extended du Pont family relocated. The company began to show a profit by the end of the War of 1812. The success of the company could be attributed in part to the efforts the du Pont brothers made to ingratiate themselves into American society and culture. Americans had become wary of French revolutionaries during the Reign of Terror and created a hostile environment for French *émigrés*. Victor and E.I. sought out opportunities to demonstrate their allegiance to America, including becoming American citizens.

Well-educated and opinionated, Josephine left behind numerous documents that provide insight into her reactions to emigrating to America and her perceptions of the early national period. Her first memoir, *Souvenirs de Madame Victor Marie du Pont de Nemours,* sheds light on her French cultural identity. [4] The correspondence illustrates her resistance to becoming American. Her second memoir, *Notre Transplantation en Amérique,* suggests that her interests focused not only on raising her family but exerting her influence over the family business and du Pont legacy.

Josephine's longing for France

During her first trip to America, Josephine arrived in Charleston knowing that her stay would be temporary. Although armed with this knowledge, her initial reactions proved to be negative. The surviving letters contrast sharply in tone to those that Victor wrote. Both Victor and Josephine compared American life to French ways, but Josephine did not celebrate America as Victor did.[5] Whereas Victor wrote to his father and described the house and servants they were able to afford, Josephine focused on negative elements. She expressed surprise that everything was so expensive, particularly the costs to move and to furnish their home in Charleston.[6]

Another point of complaint for Josephine was fashion, revealing again her longing for France. "Women dress with a British style here even more than in Philadelphia [...] You would not believe how the French style is discredited here."[7] The lack of enthusiasm for French fashion could have been attributed to the strained political and economic relations between France and America that caused delays and cancellations in the shipment of goods.

Even more striking is the tone of sadness and loneliness that pervade her words. The toll of motherhood and the lack of close family and friends filled her letters. Two weeks after her first daughter Amelia was born, Josephine wrote, "This darling infant will fill the emptiness that I feel in the middle of all of this [...] My husband is almost all the time occupied with business."[8] A closing remark in this letter reveals her homesickness for France and for the life of the privileged classes before the Revolution. "Here one gives all to luxury [...] I compare often the life that we would have led in Paris as seen before the Revolution [...] with a charming house well furnished."[9] These sentiments reverberate in many of her writings.

The move to America, motherhood, and the loss of her former life deeply affected Josephine. She found, however, two ways to deal with this melancholy. She began to write her first memoir, *Souvenirs,* and she made an acquaintance with an American Francophile, Mme Margaret Manigault, who would remain a close friend and confidant.

Josephine asserts her French identity

Souvenirs provides insight into Josephine's initial trip to America. Generally, in this memoir, Josephine communicated to her intended audience information regarding her lineage and provided guidance to her children. However, she also revealed how she used this memoir to sustain her cultural identity. By choosing to focus on her childhood and her life in France, she constructed herself not only as a woman but, most importantly, as a *French* woman.

As Linda H. Peterson posits in her study, *The Tradition of Victorian Women's Autobiography,*

> The memoir—domestic in focus, relational in its mode of self-construction—allowed women to write as mothers, daughters and wives. It allowed them to represent their lives in terms of good feminine plots. But it did not allow them to develop—or disturb—the primary masculine tradition of autobiography, the public *res gestae* account of professional life or the more introspective developmental form of an intellectual career.[10]

Josephine employed this form to construct an identity for herself as a wife and mother but also exceeded Peterson's modest expectation by seeking to construct her identity as a French person through this medium. When confronted with American culture, the loss of the *ancien régime* culture and the responsibility for her children's upbringing, she sought to confirm her aristocratic French identity that had been formed within *ancien régime* culture. She began her memoir with a full description of the town where she was born and provided extensive details of her lineage, including the ties her grandparents had with court society. Providing the family lineage is indicative of many aristocratic memoirs of the day. Thus, while her description is not noteworthy historically, it should be acknowledged that Josephine not only considered her own background important, but also included the numerous aristocrats that she came to know while growing up in France. Josephine also justified her marriage into a non-aristocratic family: "Nevertheless," she wrote, "I was allying myself to a family made quite illustrious by its senior member."[11] It seems Josephine felt she needed to explain her associations with people of non-aristocratic background as well as emphasize her French national and cultural identity by embedding herself in the history of *ancien régime* France.[12]

In addition to the pride that she took in emphasizing her noble background and acquaintances, Josephine reasserted her political affiliation with the monarchy of the *ancien régime*. Critical of the Revolution,

Josephine expressed "an admiration that I have always held for the unfortunate Queen [Marie-Antoinette] in spite of the dreadful calumnies that darkened her life."[13] She described the Reign of Terror and demonstrated her hatred towards the revolutionaries and what they did to her France.

> The long and sinister course of the Revolution was almost at its height [...] During this time of shameful proceedings and National mourning this beautiful country presented a scene of general destruction of all law and order both moral and physical.[14]

These memoirs reveal Josephine's firm sense of a public identity in the *ancien régime*. In a post-revolutionary world, she still felt strongly about her political affiliations and confidently proclaimed her ideas by committing them to paper. This behaviour was not unusual for elite women in the eighteenth century, as Jeanne Boydston asserts. She argues that elite women in colonial and post-revolutionary America dwelled within both the public and private realms of society. The household reflected this convergence of two worlds. Primarily a place for family activities, it came to be a place for civic meetings or a venue for the production of goods to be sold as well. Women took on various roles in this vague configuration of space. They often "helped to establish and maintain trade connections and entered into the management of estates, keeping accounts, managing correspondence."[15] Society accepted this ambiguous role for elite women. Jan Lewis observed that "women's association with the household as 'wives' did not necessarily disqualify them from political identities since the conjugal unit served as the ideal for political as well as familial relationships."[16] Most importantly, Boydston argues that it was a woman's economic status that enabled her to exist in such an undefined space. The elite woman had time and resources to engage in political discussions and perhaps the desire and education to write about them.[17] Josephine illustrates the type of woman described by Boydston. She was well-educated, she wrote two memoirs as well as several other works such as treatises discussing youth, American education and native Americans, and she engaged in both the public and private aspects of life.[18]

Josephine's refusal to relinquish her French identity exemplifies Carolyn Lougee Chappell's findings on immigrant experiences. Chappell has compared two escape accounts written by a mother and daughter who left France and discussed the varying perceptions the women had of the experience. In response to these two accounts, Chappell "challenge[d] the assumption implicit in the conventional dualism of a smooth transition from expatriate to immigrant."[19] She considered instead two categories: exile and *émigré*. An *émigré* is a person who "finds a stable identity within the diaspora, within the expatriate community of persons, sharing French culture even outside the geographic space that gave rise to that culture."[20] Exiles, she asserted, are persons who "might lose that sense of belonging and need to redefine their identity without, however, necessarily making an effort to integrate themselves into a new host society, thus becoming exiles and not immigrants."[21]

Throughout her correspondence with Mme Manigault, Josephine provides numerous examples of how she remained separate from American society, placing her within Chappell's category of exile.[22] Josephine consistently separated American and French societies, underlining her reluctance to integrate into American culture. In January 1803, she described the marriage of Mr Short, an American diplomat to France, to the Duchess de la Rochefoucault and concluded, "Our French society has made an excellent acquisition."[23] In 1804, she highlighted the French qualities of Jerôme Bonaparte's American wife. "She is pretty and speaks French well."[24] And, she commented on the distinct French community, "we again have a basis of a French society but it resembles the well to do from Martinique."[25] Her correspondence includes mostly letters between Josephine and other French people living in America. One may conclude that her contact with France remained limited to perfunctory letters to her in-laws.

Josephine made great efforts to develop social relations that centered around French culture. Additionally, she endeavored to retain a physical French appearance. Betty-Bright examines Josephine's aspiration, through fashion, to appear French to American society and ultimately retain her French identity.[26] In many of the letters that Josephine wrote at the beginning of the nineteenth century, she discussed fashion with Mme Manigault. In May of 1800, she complained that the stores were poor and lacked fabric selections.[27] She extolled the beauty of a French bonnet a few years later. "I love the merits of the French model and know about the effect and the execution in having one in about the same style. The bonnet is [...] very delicious and I don't regret the price."[28] In 1818, she wrote to Mme Manigault and mentioned that she had bought some jewellery and wanted to have the family's coat of arms engraved upon it. Again, her actions reinforced the fact that she never relinquished her French identity, especially since at this time her husband had successfully demonstrated his allegiance (and subsequently his family's) to America. To conjure up images of French nobility and lineage seems on Josephine's part to be very bold.[29]

In her family life as well, Josephine continued to maintain her French identity and her status as an exile. For example, she did not agree with the way American children were educated; she felt that American education stressed the importance of business and ignored the arts. She also criticized Americans for spending far too little time raising their children.[30] Josephine sent her daughters to a private girls' school in Philadelphia directed by Mme Rivardi, widow of a French military engineer.[31] Interestingly, she supported her husband and had her sons educated in American schools.

Her choices reveal her expectations for each gender. In the private school, which emphasized French language and culture, the girls remained immersed in the culture which dominated their childhood at home. Josephine's daughters did not face any pressure to become American. Their activities within the home remained supervised by close relatives and not subject to public scrutiny. It was assumed, however, that her sons would eventually be involved in the family business and would need to know how to function in American public life. Thus, their formal education needed to prepare them for it.

Josephine's comments in her letters also suggest that her immediate family was fractured along cultural lines. She categorized her sons according to their French or American characteristics. "Alfred is the one out of our children who seems to be most inclined towards the French; it is not the same with Charles, he is very American."[32] A difference in cultural identity was most obvious between husband and wife. While Victor may have had personal sentiments towards his land of birth, he strove to demonstrate to the American public that he allied himself with America partly at least to preserve the family business in the face of tremendous anti-French sentiment. For example, he renounced his French citizenship to become a naturalized American citizen and enrolled one son in the American navy. Josephine, enmeshed in the private life of the du Pont family, had no external pressure to demonstrate an allegiance to America. As she described her political perspective to a friend,

> I am much more occupied with the events in France than those in America, but I forget that it is here that is [her husband's and children's] home [...] I have given up looking for them to detach themselves from America, it is too much to force something that is natural.[33]

Victor also recognized that his spouse had a different national identity. Josephine quoted him as saying, "I have a huge business [...] in this country but I also have a wife whose fancy it would be to see again one last time her country before dying."[34] One letter in 1814 reiterates

Josephine's view of herself as an exile; she wrote, "I stay in a country that is not my own."[35]

Josephine retains her French identity

Even though Josephine explicitly demonstrated a French identity both culturally and politically, she never had to justify it or defend it as Victor did. A main reason for this concerns her gender. At this time, society did not acknowledge women as having a political capacity. Under the legal status of *femme covert*, women were considered residents of a state but not citizens. Linda Kerber explores this issue of women and national identity. Through the court case of Martin vs. Massachusetts, Kerber illustrates how the legal status of couverture limited the political rights of women. "Couverture [was] the system of law that transferred a woman's civic identity to her husband at marriage, [and] gave him use and direction of her property throughout the marriage."[36] With this prevailing understanding regarding American citizenship, it would seem that Josephine's cultural and political identity remained a non-issue. The fact that Victor acknowledged her associations with France and labelled it "her" country is thus clarified. By the early nineteenth century, Josephine had not actively engaged in public activity and consequently never posed a threat to the family business. Privately, however, she remained vocal about her opinions because at this time, as a woman without political capacity, she was not considered a threat to American politics or society.

The Martin vs. Massachusetts case exemplifies how the political culture of America had changed from colonial times. Prior to 1800, elite women had a more ambiguous role within society and in antebellum America the accepted place for a woman was in the private realm. Boydston attributes this shift to the presidential election of 1800. She argues that with the election of Thomas Jefferson, the conservative, elite policies of the Federalist party which accepted an undefined public role for women had been replaced with the precepts of Jeffersonian Republicans who defined the public arena as strictly white and male.[37] Boydston's thesis and Josephine's experience provide clear evidence that men claimed a national identity while engaging in public activity and women were entrusted with the perpetuation of cultural identity which existed in the private realm, a space not vulnerable to public scrutiny.

According to Kerber, in the 1830 court case of Shanks vs. Dupont, the issue of women's citizenship resurfaced .[38] This case was about inheritance rather than confiscation. The Shanks case turned on the question of the allegiance of Ann Scott Shanks. She was born in the colonies, a subject of the King, married a British officer in 1781 (before the war's end, while American claims to independence were therefore in some doubt) and returned with him to England.[39] Shanks' heirs attempted to claim her American property under the terms of the Treaty of 1783.[40] The case revolved around these questions: was she to be treated as a British subject toward whose claims for property the United States was neutral; was she a *femme covert* with no legal status or property rights as an American citizen; or was she to be considered an American citizen who had renounced her allegiance? [41]

Kerber concludes that Supreme Court Justice Joseph Story brought the issue of women's citizenship to a closure. He denied that

> her situation as a *femme covert* disabled her from a change of allegiance. [He] concluded that [...] Shanks, whom the British government had never ceased to treat as a British subject, was a British subject and that her heirs could claim her property under the terms of the Treaty of 1783.[42]

Kerber considered the implications of Story's resolution. Couverture did not "undermine the political rights of women and the woman with political capacity was a woman who could choose not only her husband but also her political allegiance. She would become an alien only by an intentional act, not because [she was a woman]."[43]

In later years, as the political capacity of women broadened, Josephine continued to identify culturally and politically with France. The resolution of the Shanks vs. Dupont case led logically to the conclusion that a woman had the capacity to choose to become an alien; the converse was also true that a woman had the ability to choose to become an American. None of Josephine's family members coerced her to reject her French identity. By 1830, the du Pont family had integrated into the cultural and political fabric of America. The business, in the hands of her brother-in-law, E.I., and her son, Charles, began to thrive; the du Ponts' allegiance to America was assured. Josephine's identity with France remained unchallenged.

Josephine asserts a public identity

In addition to identifying culturally and politically with *ancien régime* France, Josephine also continued to believe that as an elite woman she was not restricted to the private realm of society. The correspondence between Josephine and Mme Manigault suggests that Josephine made no effort to conform to what the nascent American culture expected of women. For example, she never became what Linda Kerber called a "republican mother," one who accepted her role in the private sphere and sought to serve her country through patriotic education of her sons.[44] At times, however, Josephine revealed in her letters her desire to participate in the public life of the family as well. She contributed to making decisions about the business and provided money for it.

Josephine began her second memoir, *Our Transplantation to America,* in 1827, the year her husband died, and finished the last chapter in 1833. This unpublished document illustrates the fine line Josephine lived between the private and public spheres of the du Pont family. Even though Americans had adopted a more finite definition for women in the nineteenth century, Josephine did not subscribe to this trend completely. Her memoir reveals how she vacillated between a private and public life. For Josephine, the ambiguities of late eighteenth century views of women's roles persisted. While she stated several times in other correspondence that she did not feel it appropriate for her to criticize the family's business plans, in this memoir she did. Additionally, the fact that she addressed the memoir to her sons and nephews on the first page suggests that she never intended to be silent or passive regarding the public activities of the du Pont family.

The beginning of the memoir describes the family's departure from France in 1799. Her tone was negative and full of foreboding and it is useful to compare this memoir to that of the letters she wrote at the time of the du Pont family's departure from France. In 1799, she seemed confident about the family's future. Her reflections upon the move thirty years later expressed much regret about that decision. In the memoir, her commentary was most likely shadowed by knowledge of the fact that she and Victor had experienced great loss and disappointment in their life in America. She commented on du Pont de Nemours' original plan to move to America, "the plan was too far decided for it to be possible or even convenient to change so tremendous a project which had many weak points."[45] In retrospect, she believed that she resigned herself to move to America for a second time. "Desertion [of the family business] was therefore impossible; we must go and we left dear France again [...] on October 1, 1799."[46]

Throughout her memoir, Josephine reminded the reader of her purpose in writing. In addressing it to her sons and nephews, she clearly wanted them to understand the actions of Victor in the family business. By excluding her daughters and nieces, she insinuated that women at that time had no reason to understand or place judgment upon the business or public aspects of the family. Early on she explained,

> my children and my nephews when they look upon these memoirs will see I believe with a gentle pride that not only was the most perfect integrity

> shown deep in [Victor's and E.I.'s] hearts but that the family feeling was so fine that the best or the worst lot in the eyes of each one was only a matter of circumstances.[47]

In addition to providing an explanation to future generations of the family business, Josephine expressed her attitudes and criticisms of what occurred during their time in America. At every opportunity, she included what her own solutions to the family problems would have been. She had specific ideas on how to relieve the family of its troubles. She recalled three solutions she had suggested. They were to (1) have her go to France to recover some of the money owed to her by the government, (2) ask the American president for an appointment for Victor at home or abroad to develop some sort of commercial establishment, or (3) enter into a business transaction with the Russian government.[48] In addition to her proposals, Josephine provided practical help as well. Early on, she supplied the business with $3,000 of her own funds.[49] It is in these parts of the memoir that Josephine attempted to engage in the debates and activities of public life of the du Pont family.

At other points in the memoir, she noted her choice not to insinuate herself in business decisions. She knew that she would never have to take responsibility for the financial problems herself because as a woman, her ultimate role was to remain passive. She wrote about leaving France: "I submitted with good grace in order not to have responsibility for the consequences, which has always been a rule of conduct for me in the major happenings of my life."[50] In another instance, she again removed herself from any responsibility. "It was such a major event in our lives that I became passive to the greatest degree [...] I retired with good grace, finding that an excellent argument for submitting obediently when one is a woman is that we immediately avoid the terrible burden of responsibility."[51] The fact that Josephine made a conscious choice about whether to engage in the family business underscores Boydston's thesis that women did not have a fixed place within society.

Josephine's move to America in 1800 reveals for us how one French woman dealt with the experience of immigration. Her life encompassed many changes in politics and society; however, her identification with the *ancien régime* remained constant. This alienation from society along with her elite status led to her continued cultural identity with France. As a woman, she did not participate in public affairs, and thus her French identity never posed a threat to a hostile American society, nor did it compromise the family business. And, her husband fully supported her continued allegiance to France. One wonders how many more immigrant women felt this way.

Citizenship in the new republic was an emerging concept. For men, there were no federal regulations and the process varied from region to region. Additionally, many immigrants did not immediately seek to become citizens.[52] For women, citizenship was never an option as they assumed their husband's nationality. In America in 1800, the social and political circumstances pushed women away from public engagement. Josephine's love of France was apparent with the friends she kept, the way she dressed, and her criticism of American society, education and politics. Her memoirs provided an outlet for her to record her desires to return to her homeland. Her negative attitude towards her personal experience in America suggests that she lived as an exile in America.

As an exile, Josephine chose to maintain the national and cultural identity with which she was born. During her life, a woman's relationship with the state fluctuated. It was ambiguous prior to and immediately following the American and French revolutions. However, by mid-century, the state began to grapple with the role of the woman in public life again. Throughout these changes Josephine, supported by her education and elite status, persisted with her French identity in both the public and private realms of the community.

Notes

This paper is derived from a chapter in my dissertation. E. Spratt, "Being French in America" (PhD diss., The Catholic University of America, 2004). It was modified for the West of England and South Wales Women's History Network Conference in Bristol, England, June 23, 2007. I would like to thank Robert Schneider, Ph.D., Margaret Steinhagen, Ph.D., Susan Barber, Ph.D., my anonymous reader and Donald Spratt for their insightful comments and support.

1. Gabrielle Josephine de La Fite de Pelleport (hereafter Madame VMDP), *Notre Transplantation en Amérique,* trans. Sophie du Pont (August 25, 1833) Accession #502, DE, Hagley Museum and Library (hereafter HML) 7.
2. Madame VMDP, *Notre Transplantation en Amérique,* 57.
3. Some studies include: Bernard Bailyn, *The Peopling of North America* (New York: Knopf, 1986); Marianne Wokeck, *Trade in Strangers: The Beginnings of Mass Migration to North America* (University Park: Pennsylvania State University Press, 1999); Ida Altman and James Horn, *To Make America: European Emigration in the Early Modern Period* (Berkeley, Oxford: University of California Press, 1991). A sampling of the scholarship examining French *émigrés* in America includes: Durand Echeverria, *Mirage In the West: A History of the French Image of American Society to 1815* (New York: Octagon Books, Inc. 1966); C. Hébert, "The Pennsylvania French in the 1790s: The Story of their

Survival" (PhD diss., University of Texas at Austin, 1980); Donald Greer, *The Incidence of Emigration During the French Revolution* (Cambridge, Mass.: Harvard University Press, 1951.); Francis Sergeant Childs, *French Refugee Life in the United States, 1790-1800: An American Chapter of the French Revolution* (Baltimore: Johns Hopkins Press,1940); and Darrell R. Meadows, "Engineering Social Networks and the French Atlantic Community, 1789-1809," *French Historical Studies* 23/1 (2000): 68-102.

4. Mme VMDP, *Souvenirs de Madame Victor Marie du Pont de Nemours* (hereafter *Souvenirs*), (DE: Privately printed, 1908).

5. Victor had travelled to America on several occasions as an aide in the French diplomatic corps. His previous trips occurred between 1787 and 1793.

6. Mme VMDP to Mme Talon, November 11, 1795, The Winterthur Manuscripts (hereafter WMSS), Group 3, Series D, Box 27, HML.

7. Mme VMDP to Mme Talon, November 11, 1795, WMSS, Group 3, Series D, Box 27, HML.

8. Mme VMDP to unknown recipient, January 25, 1795, WMSS, Group 3, Series D, Box 27, HML.

9. Mme VMDP to unknown recipient, January 25, 1795, WMSS, Group 3, Series D, Box 27, HML

10. Linda H. Peterson, *The Traditions of Victorian Women's Autobiography* (Charlottesville: University of Virginia Press, 1999), 20-21.

11. Mme VMDP, *Souvenirs*, 161.

12. It is even more noteworthy that she did not consider the du Pont family to be aristocratic, as DPDN had been given a title prior to the Revolution.

13. Mme VMDP, *Souvenirs*, 146.

14. Mme VMDP, *Souvenirs*, 146.

15. Jeanne Boydston, "Making Gender in the Early Republic," in *The Revolution of 1800* ed. James Horn, Jan Lewis and Peter Onuf (Charlottesville: University of Virginia Press, 2002), 243.

16. Boydston, "Making Gender in the Early Republic," 245.

17. Boydston, "Making Gender in the Early Republic," 245.

18. Mme VMDP, "La réserve indienne," WMSS, Series D, 1806 or later, Box 33; "Quelques réflexions souvent comparatives entre le pays natal et le pays d'adoption," WMSS Series D, c.1820, Box 33; "Pensées et réflexions diverses," "De la religion et de la sagesse," WMSS, Series D, n.d., Box 33.

19. Carolyn Lougee Chappell, "'The Pains I Took to Save My / His Family': Escape Accounts by a Huguenot Mother and Daughter after the Revocation of Nantes," *French Historical Studies*, 22/1 (1999): 3.

20. Chappell, "'The Pains I Took to Save My / His Family,'" 3.

21. Chappell, "'The Pains I Took to Save My / His Family,'" 3.

22. Mme Manigault befriended Josephine when the du Ponts lived in Charleston.

23. Mme VMDP to Mme Manigault, January 3, 1803, Accession #502, DE, HML.

24. Mme VMDP to Mme Manigault, May 6, 1804, Accession #502, DE, HML.

25. Mme VMDP to Mme Manigault, January 17, 1805, Accession #502, DE, HML.

26. Betty-Bright P. Low, "Of Muslims and Merveilleuses: Excerpts from the Letters of Josephine du Pont and Margaret Manigault," *Winterthur Portfolio* Vol. 9 (1974).
27. Mme VMDP to Mme Manigault, May 18, 1800, Accession #502, DE, HML.
28. Mme VMDP to Mme Manigault, December 18, 1803, Accession #502, DE, HML.
29. Mme VMDP to Mme Manigault, January 23, 1818 and April 5, 1818, Accession #502, DE, HML.
30. Mme VMDP, "Quelques réflexions souvent comparatives entre le pays natal et le pays d'adoption," WMSS, Series D, Box 33, HML, 1830, 14-29.
31. Betty-Bright P. Low, *France Views America: 1765 - 1815, An Exhibition to Commemorate the Bicentenary of French Assistance in the American War of Independence* (Wilmington, DE: Eluthérian Mills- Hagely Foundation, 1978), 199.
32. Mme VMDP to Mme Manigault, January, 2, 1815, Accession #502, DE, HML.
33. Mme VMDP to Mme Manigault, August 30, 1815, Accession #502, DE, HML.
34. Mme VMDP to Mme Manigault, April 27, 1818, Accession #502, DE, HML.
35. Mme VMDP to Mme Manigault, 1814, Accession #502, DE, HML.
36. Linda Kerber, "The Paradox of Women's Citizenship in the Early Republic: The Case of Martin vs. Massachusetts, 1805," in *Toward an Intellectual History of Women*, ed. Linda Kerber (Chapel Hill, NC: University of North Carolina Press, 1997), 264. The court case focused on land that been given to Anna Gordon Martin by her father. In 1783, she left America with her husband, a British officer, and moved to England. The state of Massachusetts considered them traitors and confiscated their land. In 1805, her son, James Martin, "demanded the return of properties confiscated from his mother twenty years before." The resolution of the court case confirmed the lack of political rights and citizenship for women. Judge Theodore Sedgewick wrote extensively on the resolution. He posited that under couverture, a woman did not have a political capacity within the state and thus could not be considered a traitor. Therefore, her land could not be confiscated. He argued that Anna Martin had left America because she had to follow her husband.
37. Boydston, "Making Gender in the Early Republic," 259.
38. Kerber, "The Paradox of Women's Citizenship in the Early Republic," 299. It has not been established if the person named Dupont in this case was related to the family discussed in this paper.
39. Kerber, "The Paradox of Women's Citizenship in the Early Republic," 299.
40. Kerber, "The Paradox of Women's Citizenship in the Early Republic," 299.
41. Kerber, "The Paradox of Women's Citizenship in the Early Republic," 299.
42. Kerber, "The Paradox of Women's Citizenship in the Early Republic," 299.
43. Kerber, "The Paradox of Women's Citizenship in the Early Republic," 300.
44. Linda Kerber, "The Republican Mother: Women and the Enlightenment – An American Perspective," *Toward an Intellectual History of Women*, 41-62.
45. Mme VMDP, *Notre Transplantation*, 5.
46. Mme VMDP, *Notre Transplantation*, 11.
47. Mme VMDP, *Notre Transplantation*, 16.
48. Mme VMDP, *Notre Transplantation*, 47.

49. Mme VMDP, *Notre Transplantation*, 18.
50. Mme VMDP, *Notre Transplantation*, 7.
51. Mme VMDP, *Notre Transplantation*, 36- 37.
52. Marilyn C. Baseler, *"Asylum for Mankind," 1607-1800* (New York: Cornell University Press, 1998), 295.

CHAPTER FIVE

MOVED TO MINISTER: CHRISTABEL PANKHURST AND AIMEE SEMPLE MCPHERSON IN LOS ANGELES

LINDA MARTZ

In the years between 1900 and 1950, the city of Los Angeles grew from a semi-colonial outpost that was still cutting its teeth as an American city, to the fourth largest urban area in the United States. This growth was not a product of chance, but rather of a sustained, focused effort on the part of civic leaders to turn their city into a power to be reckoned with. In an era when size was the only criterion that mattered, civic leaders, or "boosters" in the parlance of the times, sought to attract ever-increasing numbers of migrants by waging intensive advertising campaigns to lure new residents. They targeted financially comfortable Midwesterners seeking optimal investment opportunities or simply a physical paradise in which to retire, but their message also reached potential migrants across the country and even around the world. As a result, the population went from just over a hundred thousand people to nearly two million in the first fifty years of the decade. Although many different groups responded to the advertised allure of the health-giving temperate climes of Southern California, this expanding population was in the early years fairly homogeneous: white, older, financially secure retired farmers from the socially and religiously conservative American heartland, often unprepared to cope with the lack of fixed social boundaries in the constantly evolving, relocated population of the burgeoning city.[1]

Women were not only widely represented in this migration but also actively courted to become a part of it. Advertising to persuade couples and families to relocate to the region often featured happy, bouncing babies or families engaged in wholesome outdoor activities. Articles touting real estate and home construction opportunities appealed directly to women, claiming that Southern California's lifestyle and domestic architecture (namely the California bungalow) made women's lives easier than anywhere else in the country. As many of the pre-Depression migrants were farm families who sought to benefit from a period of exceptional profits by retiring early and living off the rents from their Midwestern farms, the women who came often had, for the first time, fewer domestic responsibilities and thus much more free time than they had when running farm households.[2]

While some women were being sold the transition from farm wife to lady of leisure, all female migrants understood that an even more radically life-changing experience could await them in Southern California: discovery by Hollywood. As both film and mainstream magazines assured them, all it took was being in the right place at the right time and anyone could be transformed into a goddess of the silver screen. Whether drawn to the region by the promise of fame and glamour or led to believe that transformation by fame and glamour was an integral part of their newly adopted local environment, migrants had expectations of and attitudes towards celebrity that left significant scope for recognition of women of prominence or, at least, for women made prominent by the media.

It is this confluence of an uprooted population seeking direction, of a media-based social and economic local culture, of expectations of women's advancement through media exposure, and of wide-ranging changes in religious practice that made possible new careers for two women, not usually seen first as migrants but both migrants nonetheless: Aimee Semple McPherson and Christabel Pankhurst. Both women had already achieved a certain prominence before their arrival in Los Angeles, the former as an itinerant preacher and healer and the latter as a leader of the British militant suffrage movement, but both settled in the region to take advantage of opportunities made possible by heady changes bringing together female celebrity, expanding media, and new spiritual practices. The Fundamentalist Christabel Pankhurst used her university training, feminist orientation, and long years of political debate to argue that the hallmarks of modernity fulfilled the Biblical prophecy of Christ's return; doors were opened first to the former suffragette and then to the well-travelled, well-read British preacher. Canadian Pentecostalist Aimee Semple McPherson had crisscrossed North America as an itinerant evangelist before hearing God's call to evangelise Los Angeles. Her Pentecostal experience had pushed her to think across gender and racial boundaries, endowing her with the authority needed to assemble around her not only an extensive congregation but also a large denominational structure with outreach to the marginalized populations of Hispanics, African-Americans and poor people displaced by the Great Depression. These were all populations that civic leaders preferred to ignore. Both women preached positive Christian messages that differed from those of their male counterparts, and both used their mission to address socio-cultural conflicts that their male counterparts seemed unwilling to engage with constructively. As new Angelinos, migrants seeking to reinvent themselves in a city where nearly everyone was a migrant seeking to reinvent him or herself, and as media-prominent women in a time and place where more women were free to support female-led activities, McPherson and Pankhurst were both able to overcome gender-based limitations and establish successful careers.

Religious regional culture and evangelical Protestant change

Southern California in the interwar years thus found itself with significant numbers of women from the religiously conservative American heartland, sometimes older and ailing, often with time on their hands, lacking purpose or direction, and seeking the means to adjust to new lives without the social and moral cues provided by their smaller, more settled communities. It seems legitimate to conclude that this was a major factor in one of the often-commented-upon developments stemming from this period of migration: the rise of a rather peculiar religious culture. Its hallmark was its quirky variety, as scholars and novelists alike have observed, often with scorn. One example, from *The New Republic* of 1927, suffices:

> There is an office building in Los Angeles which is devoted exclusively to these new and errant sects. While the leisurely elevator creaks upward, you may see a veritable congress of religions gold-lettered on the doors – "Children of the Sun Church," "Nature's Way Medical College for Drugless Healing," "The Vedantic Brotherhood, Hours 10-12, 2-4," "The Light, the Key and the Path, Editor's Office," "Pre-Astral Fraternity of Love." What opportunities for learning all the mysteries of the universe, all the secrets of success, the elevator boy confronts every day! … and misses, if we may judge the shabby, hang-dog look of him.[3]

While it is easy to dismiss such comments as exaggerated, 850 of the 1,833 houses of worship in Los Angeles were neither Protestant nor Catholic in 1946, a moment by which the Great Depression and the Second World War had dampened some of the city's earlier religious excesses.[4] Certainly during the interwar period new residents seemed to experiment with religious practice just as they experimented with new ways of living in the seemingly limitless sunshine of their new environment: only one in five in 1927 was regularly affiliated with a congregation.[5] Whereas traditional Protestant practice had made church-going a primary means of socializing and spending leisure time in the small towns and provincial cities from whence so many migrants came, in Los Angeles different faiths competed with each other as well as with secular distractions to capture public attention, and faith and entertainment often seemed intertwined. At the same time, American Protestant practice itself was undergoing significant changes. In addition to the challenges faced by rapid urbanization, Protestantism was still coming to terms with the paradigm shift brought on by Darwinism, as the 1925 Scopes trial, pitting evolutionists against creationists, highlighted. The liberal response intended to "modernize" Christian theology triggered the rise of a number of evangelical movements that sought to counter this impulse and to reassert biblical inerrancy and salvation through a passionate, often physical experience of divine grace. Given its tolerance for unusual or innovative religious practice and its newly-relocated, traditionally religious Mid-Western population, Los Angeles became, not surprisingly, one of the national centres for two such movements, Fundamentalism and Pentecostalism. As such, Los Angeles came to be home to two internationally prominent female preachers, one from each of those currents, both migrants in search of ministries.[6]

Before looking more specifically at the ministries of these two women, it might be useful to examine very briefly the origins and meanings of the Pentecostal and Fundamentalist movements and their connection with Los Angeles. Pentecostalism is a form of Evangelicalism that places a heavy emphasis on the personal, physically disempowering but spiritually overwhelming reception of divine grace, known as the "baptism of the Holy Spirit." This gift, like the gift of divine healing, signifies to believers that the age of miracles described by the Bible is not over: what was given by God then can be received today. Although there are recorded instances of earlier congregations being "slain by the Spirit," the modern Pentecostal movement is generally considered to be the outgrowth of a religious revival that began in Los Angeles at the Azusa Street Mission in April of 1906, at which individuals who claimed to have been "filled by the Holy Spirit" lost physical control of their bodies and began "speaking in tongues." As the movement grew, baptism of the Holy Spirit, with its accompanying gift of tongues or glossolalia, became a central signifier of the true believer, as essential as personal salvation, and belief in divine healing and the imminent return of Christ: these four tenets would become the basis of McPherson's Foursquare Gospel. The Azusa Street congregation was African-American but soon, albeit briefly, became racially diverse, a remarkable feat in and of itself for that time and place.[7] In Pentecostalism's initial period, women also led many congregations: as in earlier Holiness movements, such as the Salvation Army, God's gifts were seen as being sent to both men and women, allowing Pentecostal women a greater prominence than was possible for them in mainstream Protestantism.[8] By the time McPherson settled in Los Angeles, Pentecostalism had taken extensive root all across America and had formed into a distinct denomination; although widely distrusted by mainstream Protestant organizations, its charismatic influence extended deep into American Protestant culture.

Fundamentalism has close historical ties to Los Angeles as well. The name refers to a series of booklets entitled *The Fundamentals* that were produced between 1910 and 1915 at the behest of millionaire Lyman Stewart, founder of the Union Oil Company and a major player in the Southern California oil market, then the largest in the world.[9] Faced with the diversity of religious beliefs and with the pervasiveness of liberal religious criticism, conservative Protestants felt the need to articulate a basic dogma that would brook no dispute. Steve Bruce has defined it as follows: The new fundamentalist movement was marked by a number of specific beliefs and by an operating principle. One distinct belief was the proposition that the Bible was the inerrant word of God and hence that anything that challenged biblical teaching (such as Darwin's theory of evolution) was not just wrong, but sinful. Another was "premillennialism": the idea that the world would get worse before the Day of Judgement (which was imminent). Although a theological argument, this was to have important implications for political action. If life was due to become ever less pleasant until the righteous were lifted out of the world at what was called "the rapture," there was little point in engaging constructively with the world: better to remain pure and clean by remaining aloof. The operating principle was separatism. This principle was embodied in the creation of a series of alternative institutions: not only congregations and sects but also schools, colleges, publishing houses and radio stations.[10]

Following this principle, Lyman Stewart also founded other institutions, most importantly the Bible Institute of Los Angeles, known today as Biola University, in 1908. By the mid 1920s, the Bible Institute was publishing the leading western Fundamentalist journal, *The King's Business*, at well over 40,000 copies a month, and had its own radio station, Radio KTBI.[11] Although Fundamentalism would become increasingly separatist in the years leading up to the Second World War, in the 1920s many of the leading Bible Institute lights were leaders of mainline congregations – most of which, it should be mentioned, were suspicious of what they saw as the emotionalism of Pentecostalism.

Moving to minister: migration as a path to spiritual leadership

It was in this very diverse yet polarized environment that first Aimee Semple McPherson and then Christabel Pankhurst took up ministries, ministries that had begun in very distant places geographically. McPherson was born in Ontario, Canada, in 1890 to a Salvationist mother who consecrated her daughter to evangelism at birth. A brief period of adolescent agnosticism ended with her conversion by, and then marriage to, itinerant evangelist Robert Semple in 1908, a marriage that ended just two years later when Robert died of dysentery while they were both on mission in Hong Kong. She then travelled with her infant daughter to New York to be near her mother, and there met her second husband, Harold McPherson, by whom she had a son in 1913. She suffered from a deep post-partum depression, which lifted only after she recommitted her life to evangelism. She packed up a tent and her two small children and never looked back, preaching from the back of her automobile, holding interdenominational revival meetings and Pentecostal healing services, and bringing the baptism of the Holy Spirit to worshippers all across the United States.[12]

Her connection with Los Angeles was not only extensive but divinely ordained: it was there that she would fulfil her destiny as both mother and preacher. Her daughter Roberta contracted influenza and pneumonia during the epidemic following the Great War. McPherson wrote in the first of her autobiographies:

> I fell upon the floor and prayed to God to spare her life and the Lord gave me assurance that He would not only raise her up but also poured balm on my troubled heart by saying: "I will give you a little home – a nest for your babies – out in Los Angeles, California, where they can play and be happy and go to school and have the home surroundings of other children." […] He showed me that I had yielded up not only one but my two children, had travelled these many months with them from city to city, and town to town, having no home or bed to tuck them into, and that, just as He spared Abraham his Isaac, he would spare my two children […] It was all so real to me that I could almost see the little bungalow, floors, garden and all.[13]

Preaching as they went, McPherson, her children and her mother headed west, often over roads barely worthy of the name, in an automobile with primitive suspension and tyres that never went more than fifty miles without a blow-out. They arrived to find a Pentecostal community divided by doctrinal difference, and eager for the well-known evangelist to draw them together again in the spirit of the Azusa Street Revival. As Robert Epstein wrote in his biography of McPherson, "[At her first meeting,] she preached on the text 'Shout!: for the Lord hath given you the city.' It was prophetic." [14] Members of her new community donated the land, materials, and labour for the home that God had promised her. She used the city as a base for a series of both national and international revival campaigns, raising money to found a "center for interdenominational evangelism" that would become her permanent base of operations as of 1923. The Angelus Temple complex had a 5,300-seat auditorium, to which was added a radio station Radio KFSG in 1924 and the LIFE Bible College in 1925. She became the first woman to preach on the radio and the first to hold a radio broadcasting licence. The standing-room-only attendance at her sermons was barely dented even by her month-long disappearance in 1926, reported by McPherson as a kidnapping but claimed by others to have been a romantic tryst. A visit to Los Angeles was considered incomplete without attending one of her "Illustrated Sermons" (religious services in which were embedded staged, theatrical performances) at the Angelus Temple, and McPherson became a magnet for tourists and worshippers alike until her death from an accidental overdose of sleeping pills in 1944. Angelus Temple would become the cornerstone of a new denomination distinct from Pentecostalism and its physical exuberances, the International Church of the Foursquare Gospel, with a worldwide ministry that continues today. [15]

Christabel Pankhurst, of course, came from even further afield, both geographically and spiritually. With the exception of the years spent obtaining a law degree from Victoria University, Manchester, Pankhurst had spent virtually her entire adult life as one of the leaders of the suffrage organization the Women's Social and Political Union, a lifestyle as itinerant as that of any evangelist. The close of the First World War, however, found her despairing of the future:

> When the acute danger of the earlier months [of 1918] were over, with the Allied Armies on their way to victory, one could review the experience of the War, and, in light of it, envisage the future […] Considering the issues, the events, and the currents and cross-currents of the War, and relating it, also, to the history of times past, and having regard to the way things go and have gone, even in times of peace, this is what I realized as I never had

> realised it before: It is not laws, nor institutions, nor any national or international machinery that are at fault, but human nature itself [...] Dark, dark was the future as I looked into a vista of new warfare, with intervals of strain, of stress, of international intrigue, of horrible preparations and inventions for slaughter.[16]

During that time her wide-ranging and voracious reading led her to the work of Henry Grattan Guinness, a writer of historicist Biblical prophecy,[17] about whose work she wrote: "My practiced political eye saw that this Divine Programme is absolutely the only one that can solve the international, social, political or moral problems of the world."[18] As Timothy Larsen, the only scholar ever to study Pankhurst's ministry, describes, Pankhurst eventually sought introductions with prominent Fundamentalists, starting with F.B. Meyer in 1921.[19] Meyer was an important figure in the British Advent Testimony movement and the director of the Evangelical publishing house, Morgan and Scott, that was to publish her first book, and it was through him that Pankhurst became connected with Fundamentalist networks across North America.[20] She began her religious speaking career shortly after moving to Toronto in 1923, the year in which her first book of Biblical prophecy appeared. That volume, *"The Lord Cometh": The World Crisis Explained*, was followed by three more books of the same nature over the following seventeen years; she also wrote numerous articles, regular newspaper columns, and even briefly edited her own journal. Pankhurst's life remained very nomadic throughout the 1920s, including periods of residence in Southern California, Canada, Bermuda, the UK, and even a brief stint in the south of France that included an unsuccessful attempt at running a tea shop with her mother, Emmeline Pankhurst, and former WSPU secretary Mabel Tuke. Pankhurst appears to have spent most of the decade after her mother's death in 1928 evangelizing in the UK for the Advent Testimony movement, after which she settled permanently in Los Angeles sometime in the early 1940s.

After her conversion, Pankhurst regularly returned to Los Angeles, a Mecca of transience. Her first visit to the city was as a visitor in the winter of 1921-22, after her conversion but before beginning her ministry. During that winter, she spoke in a variety of venues on women's issues, trying to earn a living as public speaker but apparently lacking the fire that had come to be expected of the former militant leader. A leading local journalist, Alma Whitaker of the *Los Angeles Times*, had written with approval of the pre-war suffragette movement. In 1921 she met Pankhurst and observed with evident disappointment that Pankhurst had become "sweetly, passively, gently neutral," and claimed when pressed that the only solution to the world's problems was "understanding and cooperation," for which religion "was so necessary."[21] David Mitchell, in his extremely harsh biography of Pankhurst, has belittled this phase of her life, implying it to have been one long string of women's club speeches, but this is to ignore two significant points. [22] First, club life in Los Angeles at that time was incredibly dynamic and diverse as locals sought to create structures which would stabilize a rootless community. Pankhurst's contacts would have been with a wide range of women in a context that was both defining local social priorities and drawing together people as rootless as she herself was, elements that probably contributed to her choosing Los Angeles as a permanent base later on. More importantly, Fundamentalist culture was flourishing: given her beliefs, she is likely to have read *The King's Business* and listened to Radio KTBI. Thanks to F.B. Meyer, she would have had contact with the Bible Institute, and through it local Protestant leaders of many denominations, men who opened their churches to her when she returned in the spring of 1924. In that year, she gave a series of free evening lectures at the Bible Institute auditorium that ran from 27th April to 11th May.[23] At the invitation of the Reverend J. A. Hubbard, she preached two sermons on 4th May, the afternoon one based on the text "This Same Jesus Shall Come" and the evening one entitled "Some Signs of the Times," at the Church of the Open Door, an interdenominational Evangelical church founded by R. A. Torrey, the first dean of the Bible Institute.[24] That environment must surely have been influential as she published her first book of Bible prophecy the year following that stay. She was back again in California in the winter of 1931, speaking on the Second Coming at many venues, both religious and secular, and again in 1932, when she spoke only in churches and at the Maranatha Bible Seminar, a religious retreat in the redwood forests near Monterey Bay. When she returned in 1943, it was to stay. By then she had become such a feature of local life that even the often acerbic Alma Whitaker came round, characterizing Christabel as "no ranter," and her sermons as "spiritual, lucid, gently reasonably, and obviously spoken in abiding faith." [25]

Interestingly, Pankhurst's initial outings as a preacher in Los Angeles in 1924 took place during the first months of KFSG, the Angelus Temple radio station that featured McPherson's sermons and carried them, in that time of uncrowded airwaves, far across the Pacific and deep into America's heartland. We cannot know whether Pankhurst listened to KFSG, but it would have been difficult for her not to notice that McPherson was adding to her media prominence by becoming the first woman radio evangelist, and a highly successful one at that. The impact of this cannot have been lost on Pankhurst as her most interesting mark on local religious culture was to be as a radio personality. The first instance I have been able to find of her preaching on the radio in Los Angeles was in January of 1931, when "Christabel Pankhurst L.L.B, Formerly Militant Suffragette Leader of England" spoke at Calvary Church, Placentia, with a retransmission over Radio KGER.[26] This too would most likely have been though her Bible Institute connections: Calvary's founder and the pastor who invited her was Dr. Charles Fuller, who would later found the Fuller Seminary of Los Angeles and who would become a religious radio personality in his own right in 1937.[27] In 1943 Pankhurst was given her own half-hour weekly radio show on Radio KMTR, a station which had no religious affiliation and which produced a variety of entertainment programmes. Radio KMTR purchased regular well-placed newspaper advertising for the programme (outside corners in the *Los Angeles Times*) and does not appear to have bought advertising for any other religious programme. Pankhurst was obviously the draw: her name appears in what is usually one of the largest typefaces on the page, as prominent as that of McPherson or of local male religious celebrities such as Robert Schuler or Don Householder. Like most of her other writing, her programme looked at current events and analysed them as harbingers of the return of Christ. With topics such as "Christ's Return as a World-Wide Message" and "Telling All the Nations that Christ Will Return," she sought to connect the upheaval of global conflict with the Christian promise of a better world, a message that would have been especially effective in wartime Los Angeles.[28] When her programme began in September 1943, the city was swamped with military personnel and migrants in search of war work, torn by racial tensions and still reeling from the violence of the "zoot suit" anti-Latino race riots of March 1943, and expecting attack by Imperial Japan at any moment, its own residents of Japanese ancestry having been "relocated" to internment camps the year before.[29] The show ran from September 1943 to March 1944 when, at the age of sixty-four, she seems to have retired. It is interesting to note that the newspaper advertisements for her programme often shared the page with adverts for Aimee Semple McPherson's broadcasts on Radio KFSG, some of McPherson's last before her death in 1944.[30] Among the rich array of religious radio offerings to be expected in a city that was both a religious and media capital, theirs were the only women's voices.

What they both said and how they said it was affected by their status as migrants in a city of migrants and as women in a field dominated by men. McPherson's message was heavily influenced by the Pentecostalist tradition of communities of faith that transcended gender, racial and economic lines; it was also characterized, Edith Blumhofer has argued, by McPherson's childhood experience in Canada, where Protestant evangelical communities were "intertwined [...] not rivals but partners in the task of infusing the culture with Christian values, upholding civil authority, sustaining the social fabric, and civilizing public discourse." [31] Her message was also one of inclusion: she recognized the pivotal role of African-Americans in Pentecostalism by commemorating the 1906 Azusa Street revival in celebrations at Angelus Temple; she preached to racially mixed audiences; her outreach work included the local Spanish-speaking community whom she addressed through interpreters. It was in keeping with her public persona as well as her own spiritual mission as nurturer of the troubled that her Angelus Temple became a centre for social work, offering food, supplies and assistance to anyone who asked regardless of race, religion or residence status, a position that brought her in direct opposition to Los Angeles civic authorities who had posted armed guards at the California border to turn back Dust Bowl migrants. She was quick to recognize the particular needs of the city for women attracted to the glamour of Hollywood but who, unable to find work, resorted to bartering or selling their bodies. Rather than condemn and ostracise them, McPherson routinely housed unwed pregnant girls in her own home, putting them up in her daughter's bedroom.[32] Hers was a much-needed message during the Great Depression and one which made civic leaders uncomfortable. By its recognition that the social fabric was in dire need of strengthening, it was in direct contradiction with civic leaders' own propaganda of Los Angeles as an earthly paradise for retirees and investors, free of vice, poverty and racial tension. Certain aspects of her ministry were obviously present in the movements with which she had previously been affiliated, namely the Pentecostals and the Salvation Army, but no one before her combined them with such a gentle, inclusive Christian message.

Interestingly, many of her followers probably never thought of her as Canadian. Her accent, something of a mid-western twang with strongly-articulated consonants and an occasional north-of-the-border vowel, defied specific localisation and her message transcended national boundaries, but her identity was first and foremost as an Angelino who belonged to the Chamber of Commerce and marched in the Rose Parade on New Year's Day.[33] Her contemporaries would not have found this odd: people often came to the city to leave behind other selves and, after all, at the time in Los Angeles almost everybody came from somewhere else. It was this openness, in fact, to personal reinvention that gave weight to her message of gentle redemption and made possible her own transition from itinerant preacher to iconic leader of a rising Protestant denomination.

It was not McPherson's Canadian citizenship that marked her as an outsider but her gender and her alternative message: a message which was in stark contrast to that of her male peers. I cannot make the claim that McPherson preached her own "feminised" Christian message, but there are intriguing differences between what and how she preached and that means and message espoused by other prominent (male) clergy of the day. Unlike the fire and brimstone of most revivalists, McPherson's message centred on salvation and redemption, explicitly rejecting threats of Hell as a means of conversion.[34] Her imagery was drawn on Christ as Lover and Bridegroom of the Church, among her preferred texts was the sensual Song of Solomon; her publication, *The Bridal Call,* even carried a verse from the Song of Solomon on its masthead: "Rise up, my love, my fair one, and come away." She surrounded herself with flowers, always appearing with a bouquet of roses draped on her arm, and often evoked fragrance and scent, sensual responses. Her approach was motherly or sisterly: in her autobiographies she recounts drumming up interest in her meetings at secular locales ordinarily shunned by Fundamentalists, such as boxing rings and night clubs; she did this not by warning audiences there of the dangers of such earthly pastimes, but instead by issuing invitations full of warmth and humour to invite her hearers to remember their spiritual lives and attend her meetings. She was adamant in her refusal to resort to public attacks on any individual, in stark contrast to her greatest opponent in Los Angeles, Reverend "Fighting Bob" Shuler of Trinity Methodist Church, who took every occasion to denounce her, and even to her (female) associate pastor, Rheba Crawford, who, to McPherson's distress, attacked city officials when she took the pulpit during McPherson's absence.[35] She was able thus not only to embody the message of loving co-existence she preached, but also avoid accusations that her spiritual leadership had not detracted from an appropriately feminine demeanour.

If her gender influenced her message, it was certainly instrumental to her self-presentation. Early in her career McPherson kept her hair long but pinned up and wore, as virtually a uniform, a plain white dress such as nurses or domestic staff of the day wore. She chose not to bob her hair marking her as a conservative Christian and her garb conveyed an image of female service. Her migration to Southern California soon made apparent, however, that competing with Hollywood stars for the public's attention might require a different strategy. Shortly after her month-long disappearance in 1926, she not only bobbed her hair but had it marcelled, and adopted a wardrobe that kept her at the height of style. Although this radical change of image shocked and alienated some of her followers, as well as appalled the treasurer of her organization, it was an effective strategy, conveying the notion that charismatic faith was not incompatible with modern womanhood and that Hollywood glamour did not have to accompany Hollywood's moral excesses.

Pankhurst came to Los Angeles much more marked as an outsider than McPherson was, far more for her level of education and her Britishness than for her gender or past as a political activist. I think it important to underline that she did not refute her suffragette experiences: she simply saw her feminist political stance as no longer sufficient. In a *Los Angeles Times* interview, she stated:

> The suffrage work is over and there is no longer any need to promote it. I believe that after a certain amount of political and governmental service, there is a higher work to be done and, right now, I am sure the world needs prophets more than politicians. The world needs ideals and hope rather than reform and that is what I have chosen for my work – to try to bring vision to the world, to turn people back to the Bible and faith in the coming of a kingdom of God on earth.[36]

Nor did her Fundamentalist listeners and readers ever see her as a recanting feminist: she was often introduced by way of her suffragette credentials and, as Larsen argues so cogently in *Christabel Pankhurst: Fundamentalism and Feminism in Coalition*, positive reception of her as a speaker and writer came in part from a perception of the suffrage struggle as a just one. It is useful perhaps to recall that some American women had been voting in federal elections as early as 1869 and in California since 1911; by the time of Pankhurst's arrival in the 1920s, suffragette tactics could still bring out the crowds, but the fact of women voting was old news.

Pankhurst's university education, wide-ranging curiosity and legal training, however, made her much more of an outsider, particularly within Fundamentalist circles. The majority of Pankhurst's articles for the suffragette newspapers *Votes for Women* and *The Suffragette* had been editorial commentary on world and current events, glossing them in feminist terms and demonstrating that existing patriarchal structures were inadequate to right the wrongs of the world; her religious writing followed similar lines: commentary on a wide range of events ranging from the political to the scientific, and seeing in them the Signs of the Times of Christ's return or proofs of Biblical inerrancy. She could state with infectious confidence that "Einstein's theory of relativity is the greatest argument ever presented for the prophesies of the Bible." [37] Also,

> The account of Creation in Genesis has been a stumbling-block to Science, but it claims reconsideration in the light of the latest thought [...] The doctrine of relativity might do something to illumine for the scientist the time references in Genesis. The constitution of matter, as now understood, was a sealed book to those who initiated the "scientific" objections to biblical statement. It is not so much the Bible, but the whole body of the sciences, and geology and biology in particular, that need review in the light of modern scientific doctrine as to the constitution of matter.[38]

Unafraid to engage with the world and explain it in her own terms, Pankhurst was, as Timothy Larsen has observed, "… determined to claim modernity for Christ and his word," thus setting her apart from the large majority of the Fundamentalist body for whom modernity was the work of the Devil. [39] It may, however, have accounted for her success as a radio personality: her message would have been far more effective with a community proud of its advanced industries and its institutions of higher education than a flat rejection of technological change and scientific innovation would have been.

Unlike McPherson, Pankhurst foregrounded her identity as a foreigner as it was for her an effective asset. It was her work in British political life that first opened doors to her and continued to be a draw for virtually all of her professional life. Her Britishness was reinforced in the eyes of the public when she was made Dame Commander of the British Empire in 1936, and articles and advertisements invariably included the D.B.E. with even more regularity than the L.L.B (*Legum Baccalaureus* or Bachelor of Laws) to which she was also entitled. Speaking as a British woman, and as one with recognized political experience, gave credibility to her discourse: her international perspective on political events lent them sophistication and perspective, and thus fortified her religious message. Her voice, of course, furthered that image. For those who attended her lectures or listened to her radio broadcasts, her voice marked her instantly, and recordings reveal an accent crisp enough to do justice to Queen Elizabeth's Christmas message circa 1957.[40]

Thus two women evangelicals who were prominent personalities with a distinctive feminist edge shared the airwaves and competed for shelf space in the bookstores of Los Angeles, and, indeed across America and through much of the English-speaking world. Both benefited from the unsettled nature of a migrant-heavy city to redefine their own lives, and the openness of the city to newcomers allowed each to adapt her own strategy of assimilation into the regional culture, one by emphasizing her specific national origin to frame the specificity of her contributions, and the other by highlighting the rural background she shared with many of her listeners/parishioners/readers to draw together rootless migrants in a common spiritual project. Their gender allowed them to claim spaces in the public and spiritual life of a city particularly open to women in media, and to carve niches for themselves that, as the city settled and become less open to both spiritual innovation and the pushing of gender boundaries, would soon disappear.

Christabel Pankhurst and Aimee Semple McPherson would undoubtedly have been aware of each other, but did they ever meet? Both left autobiographies, in McPherson's case, several autobiographies, but all of them were written with a specific didactic intention and thus have very set limits. Pankhurst's autobiography stops with the end of the suffragette movement and in any case contains little personal reflection. McPherson's autobiographies provide a wealth of personal details, but all are constructed into parables to illustrate the power of God's Divine Grace. I was in Los Angeles in the autumn of 2006 and decided to see whether any trace of an encounter between the two women could be found. The International Church of the Foursquare Gospel still occupies some of the original buildings McPherson erected. In fact, her parsonage is now the Foursquare Heritage Center. The docent for my tour of the centre told me, to my great surprise, that both McPherson's children were still living. She agreed to ask Dr. Rolf, McPherson's son, who was still active in the church community, if he recalled hearing the name of Pankhurst or ever meeting the famous suffragette; he had no memory of the name of Christabel Pankhurst, but pointed out that he would have been away at school for the period in question. An archivist for the Foursquare Heritage Center agreed to run the name Pankhurst through the Center's database: some of Pankhurst's publications had been sold in the Angelus Temple shop, indicating Foursquare acceptance of the spiritual validity of Pankhurst's writing, but there was no record of her having spoken either in the Temple or at the LIFE Bible College.[41] A few months later I again contacted the Center, enclosing a letter to be forwarded to Roberta Semple Salter, Aimee's daughter – only to learn that Salter had just passed away. So we may never know if the two women had any contact. They might very well have, as both were notable personalities who would naturally have been curious about one another, and lived in a city where introducing oneself to newcomers and strangers was very much the norm. Then again, they might not: they were on opposite sides of the doctrinal divide separating Fundamentalism and Pentecostalism, a divide sufficiently deep at the time that any contact might have been undesirable, if not distasteful. And yet: in the parsonage, designed and built as her new home by Aimee Semple McPherson during the period of Christabel's first visits to Los Angeles, there is a large stained glass window in the entryway. It bears a motto in Latin, the translation of which is Deeds, Not Words, a phrase which in the 1920s would have been known all around the English-speaking world as the motto of the British suffragettes.

Notes

1. There are several canonical works on the history of Southern California that look in some detail at its sociological composition. These include: Carey MacWilliams, *Southern California: An Island on the Land* (Salt Lake City: Peregrine Smith Books, 1990); Robert M. Fogelson, *The Fragmented Metropolis: Los Angeles 1850-1930* (Berkeley and Los Angeles: University of California Press, 1993); the multi-volume series on California by Kevin Starr. Notable period commentators include Sarah Comstock, "The Great American Mirror: Reflections from Los Angeles," *Harper's Monthly* 156, May 1928, 715-723 and Lillian Symes, "The Beautiful and Dumb." *Harper's Monthly* 163, June 1931, 22-23. The most vivid fictional portrayal of this shifting, unstable community is to be found in Nathaniel West's 1939 novel *Day of the Locust*.
2. For a discussion of the marketing and visual images of the city's publicity campaigns see Tom Zimmerman, *Paradise Promoted: the Booster Campaign that created Los Angeles 1870-1930* (Los Angeles: Angel City Press, 2008). One booster writer who regularly included appeals to women in his pieces was Walter V. Woelhke, who wrote for *Sunset Magazine*: see for example "Los Angeles – Homeland," *Sunset Magazine*, January 1911, 3-16, or "How Long, Los Angeles?" *Sunset Magazine*, April 1924, 8-11, 100-102.
3. Bruce Bliven, "City that is Bacchanalian in a Nice Way," *New Republic* 51, July 13, 1927, 199.
4. MacWilliams, *Southern California*, 270.
5. Fogelson, *The Fragmented Metropolis*, 194.
6. For analysis of the impact of the changing face of Protestantism on American culture, see George M. Marsden, *Fundamentalism and American Culture* (Oxford: Oxford University Press, 2006).
7. Edith Blumhofer, "Azusa Street Revival," *Christian Century* 123/5, March 7, 2006, 20-22.
8. Nonetheless, their activities were not completely unencumbered. See Grant Whacker, *Heaven Below: Early Pentecostals and American Culture* (Cambridge MA and London: Harvard University Press, 2001) for a more thorough discussion.
9. First edited in 1909 by Reuben Archer Torrey, who would lead or be connected to a number of prominent Los Angeles religious/fundamentalist institutions, *The Fundamentals* is a collection of some 100 essays. It has since gone through numerous editions by a variety of publishers, the most recent being the 2003 two-volume hardback edition by Baker Books.
10. Steve Bruce, *Fundamentalism* (Cambridge: Polity Press, 2000), 67.

11. Philip Goff, "Fighting Like the Devil in the City of Angels: the Rise of Fundamentalist Charles E. Fuller," in *Metropolis in the Making: Los Angeles in the 1920s*, eds. Tom Sitton and William Deverell (Berkeley and Los Angeles: University of California Press), 223.
12. Aimee Semple McPherson frequently used episodes from her own life in her sermons, refashioning them as Christian parables. Her itinerating is described at length in her autobiography *In the Service of the King* (New York: Boni and Liveright, 1927) reprinted by her own organisation's Foursquare Publications in 1988. Two notable biographies of McPherson are Daniel Mark Epstein's *Sister Aimee: the Life of Aimee Semple McPherson* (New York and London: Harcourt Brace Jovanovich, 1993) and Edith L. Blumhofer's *Aimee Semple McPherson: Everybody's Sister* (Grand Rapids, MI: William B. Eerdmans Publishing, 1993).
13. Aimee Semple McPherson, *This is That* (Los Angeles: Foursquare Publications, 1996), 143.
14. Epstein, *Sister Aimee*, 155.
15. See Epstein's *Sister Aimee* for extensive discussion of the building and operating of Angelus Temple. See Matthew Avery Sutton, *Aimee Semple McPherson and the Resurrection of Christian America* (Cambridge MA: Harvard University Press, 2007), particularly the chapter "Marketing the Old-Time Religion," for analysis of McPherson's communication style. See Blumhofer, *Aimee Semple McPherson*, for discussion of the evolution of McPherson's teaching into a distinct denomination.
16. Christabel Pankhurst, *"The Lord Cometh": The World Crisis* Explained (London: Morgan & Scott, 1923), 8-10.
17. Timothy Larsen, *Christabel Pankhurst: Fundamentalism and Feminism in Coalition* (Woodbridge: The Boydell Press, 2002), 36.
18. Pankhurst, *"The Lord Cometh"* 3.
19. Larsen, *Christabel Pankhurst*, 21-28.
20. Larsen, *Christabel Pankhurst*, 93.
21. Alma Whitaker, "Christabel in Placid Role," *Los Angeles Times*, November 28, 1921, 13.
22. David Mitchell, *Queen Christabel* (London: MacDonald and Jane's, 1977), 286-287. He also wrote in the same pages, "Los Angeles, resounding with the sex-shot gospel of Aimee Semple McPherson, was the happy hunting ground of religious freaks and charlatans."
23. "Attacks Aimed at Liquor," *Los Angeles Times*, April 26, 1924, A2.
24. "Music Week in Churches," *Los Angeles Times*, May 3, 1924, A2.
25. Alma Whitaker, "Sugar and Spice," *Los Angeles Times*, August 8, 1943, D8.
26. Church Display Ad, *Los Angeles Times*, January 17, 1931, A8.
27. Goff, "Fighting like the Devil," 220-252.
28. Church Display Ad, *Los Angeles Times*, February 5, 1944, A2; Church Display Ad, *Los Angeles Times*, March 4, 1944, A2.
29. See Kevin Starr, *Embattled Dreams: California in War and Peace 1940-1950* (Oxford: Oxford University Press, 2002).

30. *Los Angeles Times*, February 19, 1944, page A2, for example: McPherson's Illustrated Sermon "The Exchange Ship" is advertised prominently at the top of the page, while Pankhurst's radio programme, in a smaller advert but in only slightly smaller type, appears on the lower outside corner.
31. Blumhofer, *Aimee Semple McPherson*, 42.
32. All of McPherson's biographers relate this, but see Sutton, *Aimee Semple McPherson*, 62-64 for further discussion from the daughter's perspective.
33. Recordings of McPherson's sermons are still sold by her organization.
34. McPherson, *In Service to the King*, for example.
35. The Reverend Robert Shuler (no relation to current Southern California televangelist Robert Schuller) even published pamphlets against McPherson. His popular radio programme featured denunciations of city employees dabbling in adultery or breaking Prohibition, with information provided to him by a network of spies in City Hall. He was also seen as being hand in glove with former Klansman and then Los Angeles mayor John C. Porter, who "so far [...] has not refused to accede to a single important political demand openly made by [Shuler]." Duncan Aikman, "California Sunshine," *The Nation*, 132, April 22, 1931, 448. Aimee Semple McPherson, *Aimee: Life Story of Aimee Semple McPherson* (Los Angeles: Foursquare Publications, 1979), 245. This is the first publication of a manuscript that was unfinished at the time of McPherson's death in 1944.
36. "Miss Pankhurst Here: Former Militant Suffragist Announces Self as Prophet of Approaching Millennium," *Los Angeles Times*, January 1, 1931, A10.
37. "Miss Pankhurst Here," *Los Angeles Times*, January 1, 1931.
38. Christabel Pankhurst, *The World's Unrest: Visions of the Dawn* (London: Morgan and Scott, 1921) 191.
39. Larsen, *Christabel Pankhurst*, 49.
40. As on Voices of History: Historic Recordings from the British Library Sound Archive (The British Library Board, 2004).
41. Personal email correspondence with Steve Zeleny, Director of Data Archives and Research Management, International Church of the Foursquare Gospel, dated December 12, 2006.

CHAPTER SIX

WOMEN, EXILE AND ISLAM: SOME NOTES ON RECENT WOMEN'S WRITING

SHARIF GEMIE

"Mixed feelings in a messed up world" [1]

In recent years, some important commentators have stressed the potential importance of refugee communities and exiled peoples as sites for new forms of identity, for cultural hybridities which could form libertarian alternatives to a globally-imposed universalism. For example, Homi Bhabha identified a cultural zone which he termed "the third space": a post-colonial zone between the colonized and colonizer, within which subaltern groups could develop "emergent, unanticipated forms of historical agency," a place where accepted values are "reinscribed and transvalued," a challenge to "the historical identity of culture as a homogenizing, unifying force, authenticated by the originary Past."[2] Against the persistent threat of the McDonaldization of the world, one can find significant evidence of subversive and innovative blendings, whether all-girl Moroccan punk bands or the stunningly original work of dissident Iranian photographers and cartoonists.[3] Such developments are to be welcomed by anyone who cares about the future of global culture: they are small indications that suggest that an optimistic vision of a pluralistic planetary future may be justified. This essay, however, will survey some more pessimistic evidence. It will consider a zone which, at first sight, would appear to be a suitable base for forms of "Third Space" cultures, and it will suggest that successful initiatives by writers living "between cultures" to innovate and synthesize are both rarer and more difficult than Bhabha suggests.

At the same time that marginalized writers, artists and musicians struggle to find niches within and against the structures of global culture, there has also been a massive boom in women's writing about Muslim societies, often by exiled Muslim women.[4] Sometimes this resembles a radical shift from the nineteenth-century structures of discourses, where white women could claim to be the privileged observers of the intimate and domestic aspects of Muslim societies which were closed to male explorers.[5] Now, Muslim women are narrating their own experiences, often with a similar unspoken or unexplored assumption that they too have some specific, valuable capacity to document and evaluate these societies. This has led to some unexpected situations: significantly, one can now argue that the most prominent Iranian exiles in the west are women.[6] Some of their works have even become international bestsellers: Laura Bush rated Azar Nafisi's *Reading Lolita in Tehran* as nineteenth in her list of "twenty-five works to read before you're twenty-five."[7]

At first sight this seems a positive development. Too many judgements about Muslim countries have been made solely on the basis of male accounts and analyses; the addition of female voices seems entirely welcome. But, on closer inspection, there are some peculiar features about this sudden interest in women's writing: it seems based on what one observer has called an unquenchable western thirst for "hostage narratives" concerning women and Muslim countries.[8] The cultural values presented in these books are often far from the libertarian hybridity celebrated by Bhabha. Works which at first sight appear as bridges and channels of communication between east and west seem – on reflection – more like walls or dams that reinforce exclusivity in all parties.

This paper will analyse a small sample from the great flood of works that has been recently produced. It will concentrate on ten first-person, non-fictional or lightly fictionalized autobiographical works written by women from Muslim countries in the Middle East, and with some further reference to two semi-anthropological works describing women's lives in Afghanistan. Some of the authors are well-known: for example, Nafisi (author of *Reading Lolita*) and Shirin Ebadi, Iranian winner of the Nobel Peace Prize. Others, while not so well-known, have become reasonably successful writers: Chahdortt Djavann has acquired some recognition in France following her forceful interventions on debates concerning the veil; Zainab Salbi appeared frequently on the American media during the first US-UK intervention in Iraq; Ayaan Hirsi Ali became an influential commentator in political debates in the Netherlands, before leaving to join the American Enterprise Institute, a conservative think tank. Of these ten authors, five write about Iran, two about Iraq, and three comment on – respectively – Saudi Arabia, Somalia and Morocco.

An Intimate and Honest Chronicle

These narratives are not examples of innocent *reportage*. There is an obvious mismatch between their writers and audiences: if British readers wish to understand Muslim societies, then why do they not study those countries with which they have historically had the closest connections: Egypt and Pakistan? If French people are interested in similar topics, then why not study Algeria or Morocco? Instead, the most publicized countries in this recent wave of writing are clearly Iran, Iraq and Afghanistan. This suggests that these works are – in reality – deeply and inherently politicized, for these countries constitute, respectively, the country which has posed the greatest challenge to US-UK domination of the Middle East and the countries which have had the greatest experience of US-UK intervention. Each country is, of course, worthy of academic study and of more popular forms of documentation, but there remains something strange in the manner in which these books on these specific countries are so often presented as simply representing "the east" or "Islam." Publishers' descriptions leave readers in no doubt.[9] *Reading Lolita* presents "a rare glimpse, from the inside, of women's lives in revolutionary Iran"; Farmaian has written "An intimate and honest chronicle of the everyday life of Iranian women over the past century [...] the remarkable story of a woman and a nation in the grip of profound change"; *Iran Awakening* shows the reader "the truth about the position of women in a Muslim society"; Hirsi Ali "assesses the role of women in Islam both in practice and in theory"; Carmen Bin Ladin has "intimate knowledge of the inner workings of this society." The point to note here is how these works are not presented as individual voices by women with specific histories and particular insights, but as something more akin to older, Orientalist themes: there is simply one "East," one "Islam," and therefore a single woman can quite adequately represent it.[10] The most basic point – that these are autobiographies – seems to be ignored by such presentations. Whether readers have then read them in this simplistic manner is open to question; all one can say is that publishers are inciting readers to take such an approach.

The women who wrote these works have different statuses. Some are refugees in the now-classic sense of the word: Hirsi Ali and Malika Oufkir have certainly fled their countries due to a "well-founded fear of persecution." Others – Nafisi, Tajadod, Djavann – have a more complex relationship with their homelands: they maintain an itinerant, peripheral status, returning at times, leaving at others. Some, like the Iraqi Salbi, have followed unusual, twisted routes to arrive in the west. When interviewed in the USA, she suddenly realized "I didn't even know how to describe myself. I wasn't a refugee. I wasn't a tourist. I had come here as a bride, but I wasn't a wife."[11] Still others – Ebadi, "Riverbend" – remain in their home countries but often appear to be writing *as if* they were refugees: certainly, they have experienced isolation and persecution, and these works are clearly addressed to a western audience. The "exile" referred to in the title of this paper is therefore not necessarily a physical or juridical status, but something more akin to a social condition or an attitude of mind.

While the authors of these works differ significantly, their works have some common features. They are not translations: they are all written in major Western languages, and some of the authors have used assistants to help them write. They are all published in the West. They are all principally autobiographies, with some – such as Sattareh Farman Farmaian's *Daughter of Persia* or Shirin Ebadi's *Iran Awakening* – containing substantial contextualizing historical sections, while others – such as Djavann's *Je Viens d'ailleurs* [*I come from elsewhere*] – concentrating more on using the autobiographical format to present a political message. In each case this format leads to some obvious difficulties in naming names and identifying places. Each of these authors has been threatened by state authorities – Oufkir endured fifteen years of harsh imprisonment – and one readily understands that the narratives may therefore cloud over personal details at certain points. Curiously, despite the obvious political resonances of their works, all the authors are keen to present themselves as single, exceptional females, independent of any organized political forces. The titles of their works – *A Persian Childhood; Je Viens d'ailleurs; Daughter of Persia: A Woman's Journey; The Caged Virgin: A Muslim Woman's Cry for Reason; The Female Prisoner* – often reflect this focus on the personal, on female experience and on their individual status. Titles by works by western women on Muslim countries show similar tendencies: *Three Women of Herat, The Sewing Circles of Herat* and *Muhajababes* all highlight the concentration of their respective texts on specific female communities. All the Muslim authors write in the first person. The first lines often stress the author's individual presence in the book: "I was born here, I know Tehran"; "This book is for you [my daughters]"; "A little bit about myself: I'm female, Iraqi, and 24. I survived the war. That's all you need to know."[12] "My interest has been to record what happened to me – and only to me."[13] Such lines establish the work as something more intimate that the usual narrative, suggesting perhaps that the book is like a gift from female author to female reader. It is also a feature which seems designed to reassure their readers that they are not reading a politicized, constructed narrative, but something more authentic, more spontaneous and innocent. Hirsi Ali's subtitle – *A Muslim Woman's Cry for Reason* – seems to capture something significant about this pose: her work is "a cry," not a critique or an analysis; it has been produced not by a political party or a movement, but by a single female whose principal justification for writing seems to be that she is (or was) a Muslim.

There are some counter-tendencies to this stress on the personal: the titles *We are Iran,*[14] *The Veiled Kingdom, The Harem Within, Between Two Worlds* and *Passeport à l'Iranienne* [*Iranian Passport*] [15] all refer to more collective, social situations, while *Reading Lolita in Tehran: A Memoir in Books* is unusual in so forcefully stressing a literary context. The titles of Shirin Ebadi's and "Riverbend's" works neatly combine the individual and the social in a single line: *Iran Awakening: From Prison to Peace Prize; One Woman's Struggle at the Crossroads of History; Baghdad Burning: Girl Blog from Iraq.*

Given the limitations of the first-person narrative as a form, there are some surprising variations in the texts. Nafisi's *Reading Lolita* is easily the most polished, confident and sophisticated text (but what else would one expect from a professor of English literature?) Ebadi's *Iran Awakening*, while written in relatively simple language, does present ideas which are complex and politically demanding. Tajadod's *Passeport* is unusually witty. But, more importantly, each of these works speaks of a sense of pain and humiliation felt specifically by women. "To be born a female in a Moslem state was just very bad luck and no one could deny it," concludes Pari Courtauld.[16] These works deal with some harsh, brutal topics: Hirsi Ali speaks of female genital mutilation, Djavann of rape, Oufkir and Ebadi of imprisonment, "Riverbend" of war, bombing and military occupation, and several authors describe the mass casualties resulting from the Iran-Iraq war. Where physical brutality is not present, the authors evoke a powerful sense of sexual humiliation: Nafisi narrates an incident where a female academic is prevented from entering her university by an illiterate security guard because she is not following the correct dress code. Ebadi tells of her own arrest in the street for a dress code offence, and provides a genuinely interesting account of her subsequent punishment: a moral lecture by an illiterate policewoman. This strong sense of humiliation and oppression structures these works, and often makes them resemble a literature of protest or – more distantly – the "misery memoir."

Assessing Muslim Societies

Without doubt, the overall effect of these works is to present a negative image of Muslim societies, and to leave the reader with the impression that conditions for women in such societies are probably getting worse by the day. Bin Ladin is eloquent on this point: the Middle East is

> so closed off, hobbled by layers of traditions and secrecy, where appearances seemed more important than desires... Everything seemed to be *haram*, or sinful; and if it wasn't sinful, it was *abe*, shameful [...] The system that constricted all women in a mesh of restraints made every basic gesture of my life unbelievably complex [...] No books, no theatres, no concerts and no cinemas.[17]

These are societies in which "Muslim women are scarcely listened to," in which "I learnt to be silent. To not rebel. To not see, to not understand, to not feel. I learnt to be no longer what I was."[18] Such restrictions obviously affect public political life, but – more chillingly – they also affect the most intimate moments of private life. Discussing the Iranian Islamic Republic's legislation, Ebadi protests to her liberal, open-minded and loving husband: "We used to be equals, and now you've been promoted above me, and I just can't stand it."[19] Sometimes this type of feeling is expressed as nostalgia for a more liberal past: "When I was growing up, in the 1960s, there was little difference between my rights and the rights of women in Western democracies" writes Nafisi.[20] When considering the basic point of human rights in practice, these works certainly provide simple and conclusive evidence of widespread, systematic abuses, of frequent brutality and – perhaps more importantly – of the resentment and anger felt by women who suffer under such regimes.

Questions become more complex, however, when one moves from this initial, spontaneous, sense of hurt and humiliation to considerations about how to express and formulate these feelings, with a view to developing some form of political project. The authors tended to make use of two comparisons to explain the nature of Muslim societies: one chronological, one geo-political.

Frequently Muslim societies are casually described as backward. When Veronica Doubleday first wandered through an Iranian bazaar, she recorded that "I felt we had stepped back centuries in time."[21] Christina Lamb, on seeing Kabul, wrote "there was nothing modern about the city at all; on the contrary it felt like going back several hundred years."[22] Bin Ladin described Saudi Arabia as "an opaque and intolerant medieval society."[23] Hirsi Ali complains that "the mental world of Islam is a reflection of the stagnation that entrapped this religion a few centuries after its birth."[24] As a means to swiftly and dramatically convey a sense of difference, such chronological comparisons clearly work well. But they become more problematic as means by which to *analyse* other societies. Firstly, they suggest an easy narrative of progress: every society in the world has been medieval, every society must (eventually) become modern (and western?). Such simple prescriptions ignore, underestimate and confuse important issues. One should not assume that characteristics such as an absence of technological and cultural sophistication therefore allow the equation of potentially very different societies as similar. There remain fundamental differences between a thirteenth-century English village and a present-day Saudi town: using the term "medieval" to describe both confuses analysis. Bin Ladin herself notes that if modernization can be measured in terms of air-conditioning and Toyotas, then parts of Saudi Arabia count as very modern indeed.[25] Secondly, there seems a type of chronological double-standard here. In British culture "medieval" can be used to signify a type of authenticity, providing a critical contrast to the alienated societies of late modernity. This potential positive second reading of the term never seems to be applied in relation to Muslim societies.[26] Thirdly, this type of simple chronological differentiation tends to encourage equally simple generalizations about all Muslim societies as backward: a perspective that ignores the significant differences in cultural forms, religious cultures and political structures.[27]

The second common type of comparative perspective suggests a simple comparison between a good, liberal west and a bad, tyrannical east. For Bin Ladin, the USA is "a country we loved and whose values we respected."[28] "How I came to love what the West stands for" writes Hirsi Ali.[29] While trying to escape imprisonment, Oufkir longed for "America, the Rights of Man" and "France, the country of human rights."[30] Of course, admiring a nation for its commitment to civil liberties and human rights is a worthy stance. What is more worrying is the manner in which these authors construct civil liberties and human rights as forms which are in and of themselves western (or American, French or British). This leads to a more awkward political perspective, for it suggests a type of political incapacity within Muslim countries, who will be unable to climb the ladder into liberal modernity by themselves. Worse still, it therefore positions liberals and reformers as *external* to these societies, allowing for their easy isolation by xenophobic authorities.

Alongside this political admiration of western political values, many authors also signal and document a widespread admiration for western culture. Tajadod pays for a passport photograph with second-hand copies of French *Vogue*, knowing that they will be eagerly accepted by the photographers' wives. She also provides a detailed description of a fashionable shopping centre in Tehran, offering fake Vuitton, Gucci and Prada handbags, in which Italian products are automatically more expensive than those produced in Iran.[31] "Riverbend" often tries to persuade her readership of the cultural kinship between Iraqi youth and her mainly western readers. "You wouldn't believe how many young Iraqi people know so much about American / British / French pop culture. They know all about Arnold Schwarzenegger, Brad Pitt, Whitney Houston, McDonalds and MIBs... If it's any consolation, the Marines lived up to the Rambo / Terminator reputation which preceded them."[32] Oufkir similarly records the importance of French fashion magazines, and of her joy in listening to rock'n'roll on the foreign radio stations.[33] Nafisi observes her Iranian students: "for pleasure they turned somewhere else." She cites the surprisingly eclectic mixture of the Doors, the Marx Brothers and Michael Jackson as being popular, while Djavann recalls that Madonna and Pink Floyd were the favourites of her generation, and remembers how Paris was "the city of her dreams."[34] Lamb finds the undercover reading circle in Herat enjoying Shakespeare, Joyce and Nabokov alongside classic Persian poetry.[35] Such details no doubt help the western reader contextualize a foreign people and aid in the difficult process of identification. But they are also misleading when seen as a totality. Firstly, it is by no means certain that the Michael Jackson heard by a sixteen year-old girl in Tehran is *the same* Michael Jackson enjoyed by her cousin in Cardiff or Chicago: assuming that the sound, the look, the lyrics can literally be translated or transplanted over geographic, cultural and political borders is naïve and clumsy. The possibilities of a re-reading of such works by diverse audiences are under-estimated in these uncomplicated accounts which portray Muslim people merely as simple, grateful receivers of Western cultures.[36] Zainab Salbi comments on the effects of this kind of mis-representation. "The American obsession with the way women dressed helped dupe Americans into believing that because Iraqi women looked more like them, they also had greater freedoms."[37] As was the case with the chronological comparison, a simple type of shorthand reference is here being expanded into a misleading over-generalization.

More importantly, one wonders about exactly how typical are the scenes invoked in these descriptions. Are there really no indigenous cultural forms which can rival the popularity of western importations? Is not the presence of these western products often more noteworthy as dramatic exception rather than as norm?

In fact, alongside an enjoyment of some western cultural products, one finds that some of these authors sound more critical or negative notes. Farmaian criticizes the culture of Iran's nouveaux-riches in the 1970s: their "ostentatious spending was like a heady, explosive inhalant"; it is also they who were seized with "an almost delirious admiration for things Western."[38] Ebadi signals a similar critical note: the Shah's court, where "officials cavorted with American starlets at parties soaked in expensive French champagne" attracted widespread disapproval among Iranian people.[39] This resentment of the conspicuous consumption of foreign luxury items by a privileged elite was one of the root causes of the Revolution of 1978-79. Ebadi also notes that Saddam Hussein's forces attacked Iran using European and American weapons: not all western products benefit the Iranian people.[40]

This leads us to a wider point: exactly how representative are these writers? Certainly each of them has had substantial experience with the countries they describe. The publishers' descriptions constantly present them as simply voices of their people. But, in practice, there is often an ambiguity about their identity. In the case of Nafisi, for example: Is she a Muslim? Is she an Iranian? Nafisi lived for seventeen years in Britain, Switzerland and the USA before her return to Iran in 1980. Accepting her simply as the voice of Iranian women is – once again – naive and short-sighted. Similar questions arise when one considers the social position of some of the other authors. Most of these women come from elites, sometimes from extremely and untypically wealthy families. This is revealed in their domestic arrangements. Salbi refers to her maid in passing: "We went everywhere; she went nowhere."[41] Tajadod's maid, Mohtaram, provides a minor comic theme in *Passeport*: Tajadod mocks her for her refusal to throw away anything.[42] In neither work is there any serious attempt to consider the maid's view of the world: would it be compatible with that put forward by the privileged author? More significant is the basic plot of *Passeport's* narrative: Tajadod was caught out by some new rules concerning Iranian passport applications, and the narrative's main plot is her search to bypass the rules. This is a time-consuming and costly process, but it also clearly marks her out as a member of a privileged elite, quite distant from the mass of people in Iran. "Cannes seems so far away!" she muses at one point.[43] In another passage, when approaching one of the many offices she visits, she is stopped by a crowd of women in the street.

> A great black roll of cloth seemed to cover the entire street – a cloth pierced here and there by holes through which one saw arms and faces. There were hundreds of women, all wearing black chadors, sitting in

> silence on the ground, in the street. I immediately thought that it must be a demonstration organized against Bush or Israel.[44]

Her first impressions are wrong: these women form the *ordinary* queue for passport applications, the one she is seeking to avoid. Later some of these women realize what Tajadod is trying to do: one grows furious, and threatens her: “We didn’t make the Revolution so that women like you could pass before us!”[45] The distance between Tajadod and the mass of these women is obvious, and this is not some accident of the narrative, but a point which is integral to Tajadod’s work. *Passeport* asks the reader to laugh at Iranian society: its absurd rituals of *târof* (a formalistic obsession with courtesy that makes it near-impossible to pay a taxi-driver), its complex bureaucracies, its sombre, macabre cults of mourning, its grim, repressive religion... One purpose of Tajadod’s book is therefore precisely to distance herself from these cultures, to say to her western reader: I am not like *them*, I am like *you*.

None of these points invalidate Tajadod’s narrative: *Passeport* remains a witty, neatly-written, observant, imaginative work that sheds light on aspects of ordinary Iranian life which are often ignored by more pointedly politicized works. But these points do ask us to re-consider Tajadod’s own position. As she herself states, her life is very different from the life of the mass of women in Iran: it would be wrong to read her work as presenting values and attitudes which are typical of all Iranians. One could imagine other narratives: what else might we learn of Iran if *Passeport* had been written by Mohtaram, her maid, or by one of the black-clad crowd waiting in the street? While it is relatively easy for a western readership to identify with the sassy Tajadod, with the ultra-French Djavann and with the Austen and Nabakov-citing Nafisi – even Laura Bush can do that! – it is far harder to feel any empathy for the chador-wearing crowds. This leads to some very awkward questions, pointedly framed by Saïda Rahal-Sidhoum. “It is the women whose language, looks, clothes and goods are similar to those of [the west] who are listened to,” while as for those who are different “their ideas are judged to be unacceptable, as they are stained with Islamism.”[46]

Making Contact

The argument presented so far in this paper is that the process of making contact with women in Muslim societies is more difficult than often assumed, and the paths shown us by a series of relatively prominent, celebrated female writers are actually misleading and even positively unhelpful. A supplementary argument is that we have been mis-reading these works: they do not represent "the East," "Muslim society" or even Iran; while they are revealing and significant works, they are more partial, personal and idiosyncratic than is usually thought.

For some of these writers, the issue of a construction of an egalitarian and representative dialogue between east and west is simply a non-question. The assumption of the superiority of western cultural values and intellectual analyses is taken for granted; indeed the whole point of some of these works is precisely to assert and reinforce this point. Thus, for Hirsi Ali "Self-criticism for Muslims is possible in the West, because the West, primarily the United States, is waging war on Islamic terrorism."[47] While Nafisi's and Tajodod's writing is less blunt, the force of their work is to carry the same message: there is nothing to be gained from Muslim cultures, all true lovers of liberty must look to the west. As for dialogue: Tajadod passes over the issue in an indirect form. In one curious scene in *Passeport*, she watches pornographic videos from western countries with a visiting television repairman [sic], and observes "these videos give a strange image of the West, a false – even an extravagant – image, of course, [an image of a society] in which all women have only one desire: to throw themselves on any man who passes, but still an image that a great many simple people think must be true."[48] The reverse question never seems to occur to her: what will be the effect of her writing on a western audience? What impression will they get of Iran, the East and Islam? Does this matter?

Veronica Doubleday also touches on the same question in a light, indirect manner. Living in Afghanistan in the 1970s, she grew friendly with a small group of women. As a good anthropologist, she was able to overcome the many barriers of class, language, ethnicity and culture. But there still remained one uncrossable frontier: the burqa. Women "moved silently and inconspicuously, closely veiled, impenetrable and faceless. I was appalled by my first sight of the Afghan burqa."[49] Some months later, however, she makes friends with some Afghan women who persuade her to try on a chador.

> I had thought I was buying something drab and shapeless, but they made me see that the prayer veil was a highly coveted item of fashion [...] The reaction among the Herati women was unanimous: the veil looked beautiful and they were pleased that I had adopted their custom. [Yet] I do not approve of the veil, and I see it as a vehicle of oppression.[50]

On the one hand, one must congratulate Doubleday for illustrating a dilemma: when two cultures meet, but present apparently incompatible practices, how does one make contact? When is it right to just say "no"?

On the other hand, she provides no resolution. Having negotiated her way through so many barriers, Doubleday just seems to stop: East is East and West is West, she seems to conclude. The crucial question, however, remains: how can an egalitarian dialogue be created?

Some of the Muslim women authors raise exactly this type of question. "Riverbend" is quite eloquent and forceful about the persistent misconceptions that western readers often have about Iraq.

> The Myth: Iraqis, prior to occupation, lived in little beige tents set up on the sides of little dirt roads all over Baghdad. The men and boys would ride to school on their camels, donkeys and goats. The schools were larger versions of their home units and for every one turban-wearing teacher who taught the boys rudimentary math (to count the flock) and reading. Girls and women sat at home, in black burkas, making bread and taking care of 10-12 children.
>
> The Truth: Iraqis lived in houses with running water and electricity. Thousands of them own computers. Millions own VCRs and VCDs. Iraq has sophisticated bridges, recreational centers, clubs, restaurants, shops, universities, schools, etc. Iraqis love fast cars (especially German cars) and the Tigris is full of little motor boats that are used for everything from fishing to water-skiing.
>
> I guess what I'm trying to say is that most people choose to ignore the little prefix "re" in the words "rebuild" and "reconstruct".[51]

While this passage forcefully reminds readers of the need to avoid Orientalist clichés in order to understand Iraq properly, it nonetheless reinforces another point of Orientalist logic, whereby there are only two realities: the Orient and the Occident. "Riverbend's" heartfelt plea will be read by many western readers to signify that if Iraq is not *really like* the classic clichés of the Orient, then it must be *like* the Occident: an equally misleading perspective.

The process of finding a voice in the West can be more problematic than might be expected. Djavann speaks of "reconstructing her life in French."[52] For Djavann, this process was relatively successful and even liberating: for others, the process is far more taxing. One of the most basic issues relates to racial identity. Many Middle Eastern Muslims do not think of themselves as "coloured," let alone as "black." Gelareh Asayeh, an Iranian now living in the USA, notes "I grew up thinking I was white": she was surprised and disconcerted to be classified as "coloured" when she arrived in the USA.[53] Other issues are frequently raised. Farmaian, an Iranian arriving in the USA in 1945, grew tired of having to explain that she was *not* an Arab, irritated by American students' near-complete ignorance of Islam but, above all, angry about questions concerning harems. "Thanks to Hollywood, however, they had heard of harems, a topic of the greatest fascination to my fellow dormitory residents. They seemed disappointed when I explained that, although Moslems were allowed four wives, few could afford more than one. Their curiosity about this made me very uncomfortable."[54] Even apparent success and prestige in the west can often have unwelcome consequences. Marjane Satrapi, the author and designer of the extremely successful graphic novel and film *Persopolis*, notes:

> From Iranian movies, it has been inferred that Iran was a picturesque country where children ran around looking for "the house of their friend." When Shirin Ebadi was awarded the Nobel Prize, the one detail that was immediately noted was that she didn't wear the veil – which was used in France as an argument to hastily pass the law banning the veil.[55]

Alavi complains of the manner in which the western obsession with the veil obscures a comprehension of Iranian feminism. "These [Iranian] women activists are less interested in whether or not to wear the veil and more concerned with gaining access to education, wider employment opportunities, equality at work and better health care for their families."[56] Some of these travellers and exiles carry with them a sense of resentment at the way their experiences and their lives have been re-packaged in order to fit the political and cultural requirements of the western media. For them, the success of *Reading Lolita* in the west is not the equivalent of the opening of a dialogue or the beginning of an emancipatory project: rather, it is another example of a long-running Orientalist saga.

Ebadi's *Iran Awakening* responds to many of these issues. She is often sceptical, sometimes even critical, of a presumed western benevolence. She refuses to accept the principles of the west as obligatory political norms which she must revere, and instead considers that there are intellectual concepts *within* Islam on which a deep, radical reform process can be built. Ebadi is therefore an "advocate for female equality in an Islamic framework."[57] She depicts Iran as a dynamic society, and does not see her Islamist opponents in stereotypical terms as "reactionary" or "medieval": instead she locates the rise of radical Islam within a precise historical context set – in part – by Western imperialism.

Of all the works surveyed here, however, it is Salbi's *Between Two Worlds* that most clearly reveals the gap between even well-meaning western perceptions and Muslim experiences. During the first invasion of Iraq, she received widespread publicity in the American media. At first she welcomed this: as a distant relative (by marriage) to Saddam Hussein she had a very clear idea of the brutality of the regime: "I feared Saddam with every part of my body and mind and soul, and that organic fear would never leave me."[58] She shared the hopes of many Iraqis that the US-UK intervention would lead to a genuine liberation. But as her image proliferated, she began to realize that she was being exploited by the American media. She became "a kind of national poster girl for the 'Iraqi side' of the story [...] the innocent, nonthreatening Iraqi."[59] The media attention given to her personal misfortune and her relief on getting out of Iraq allowed Americans to justify a political-military intervention that seemed very far from Salbi's first hopes. This leads her to re-think many elements of her personal and political life.

After an abusive marriage, Salbi re-married. Having learnt to fear Islam, she discovered (or re-discovered?) another side to Muslim culture with her new husband. "He reintroduced me to that part of Islam that was not confused with rule-bound ancient cultures, that part of Islam that was beautiful, my mother's faith."[60] Perhaps better still, she learnt of an unexpected aspect of Islamic law: the right of a bride to make legally-binding stipulations of her husband before marriage. "Another thing we hadn't been told about in Iraq!"[61]

The fascinating point about Salbi is that within this small sample of women's writing, she is almost unique in her reactions: unlike the other writers, her final reaction is participation in a form of collective action. She joins a welfare organisation – Women for Women International – that works with women refugees and other abused women. She demonstrates a sympathy for their condition, and notes some common experience of humiliation, oppression and intimidation that transcend particular political disasters. But she also transfers some of the lessons she learnt from her experience with the American media. When working with veiled Muslim Afghan women, she remembered that "my job was to help them achieve their own goals, not impose mine."[62] Of the women of our sample, she is one of the few who espouses causes and values that could be termed feminist, and her work ends with an important statement about her public and private identity: "The last thing I would claim is to represent all Iraqi women, let alone all Arab women or all Iraqis. I am a mix of the cultures and times in which I have had the privilege to live."[63] Once again, this is an unusual and distinctive stance, which suggests how carefully Salbi has thought about her writing and how it might be read. Does this type of stance merit the term "Third Space"?

Conclusion

This analysis of a sphere of women's writing shows that many contributors find it difficult to transcend the political and cultural divisions of the "clash of civilizations." Each of our writers is a traveller, but the journeys they have made are not as straightforward or as obvious as may appear from publishers' descriptions. Many writers in our sample – Djavann, Tajadod, Hirsi Ali, Nafisi – consider that one has to choose one's camp. In these cases, their political lesson is clear: the camp of the west is obviously superior, in almost every way, to that of the east. Significantly, they are also keenest to present themselves, in the most simple terms, as representing "the East" or "Islam": the assumption is that every Muslim woman secretly wants to join Hirsi Ali's *Muslim Woman's Cry for Reason*. Their writing is something other than a necessary documentation of the grave deficiencies in the human rights record of many Muslim states: it is an asymmetrical form of writing which re-creates the power relationship between East and West. Muslim cultures are dismissed as incapable of reform or independent initiatives of their own. The spectacle of female oppression is exploited politically. "Afghan women under the oppressive rule of the Taliban swiftly became the symbol of oppression by Islam" notes Milani perceptively, "their plight perfectly captured by the metaphor of the prisoner without a chance of parole or reprieve."[64] Hirsi Ali makes clear the political implications of such a choice: "we need the help of the liberal West."[65] Each of these women has good, strong personal reasons for their choice; each can state, with the benefit of their personal experience, the real advantages that Western societies have given them. These examples show how difficult it is to realize the potential which Bhabha sees in the "Third Space." More seriously, one must further note that this "Third Space" of exiles, migrants, marginals and itinerants can also be a zone in which openly conservative and authoritarian forms of political culture thrive: one could point to both forms of Orthodox Judaism and fundamentalist Islam which have effectively exploited the opportunities of the "Third Space."[66]

On the other hand, there are also some more ambitious and demanding propositions emerging within this strand of women's writing. Such writers raise questions about easy assumptions concerning how Muslim societies should be represented. These dissidents face enormous problems in finding their space within western culture: Salbi's brief experience as a media star is an exemplary warning of how even a friendly and supportive audience can both misunderstand and actually exploit an exile's experience. Under such circumstances, creating an independent, critical voice that can speak to (at least) two different cultures takes amazing determination and skill. Ebadi won her Nobel Prize for her work on human rights in Iran: she deserves another prize for her ability to transcend the polarized political essentialisms of the "Clash of Civilizations." Both Salbi and Ebadi move beyond the autobiographical sensationalism of Djavann and Hirsi Ali: Salbi to renounce the misleading status of "a woman speaks out against Islam", Ebadi to stress the collective nature of a struggle for human rights. And yet, it must also be acknowledged that while both are competent writers with provocative ideas and interesting observations, neither of these books is a literary or political classic. Their writing lacks the excitement often associated with the concept of "hybridity": an idea which is more complex and problematic than it may seem, for it still presupposes original "essences" which must be mixed and blended to produce a new condition.[67] Perhaps the visual and musical arts, with their stress on immediate, non-verbal communication, are more appropriate places to search for the imaginative new forms of the worthy ideal of the "Third Space": the widely circulating documentary literature on women's lives in Muslim countries suggests, instead, the continuing domination of relatively conservative forms of expression.

Notes

The author would like to thank Paul Chambers, Patricia Clark, Vanessa Dodd, Louise Rees and Diana Wallace for their useful comments on this work. All translations from French-language works are my own.

1. "Riverbend," *Baghdad Burning: Girl Blog from Iraq* (London: Marion Boyars, 2006), 42.
2. W. T. J. Mitchell, "Translator translated (interview with cultural theorist Homi Bhabha)", http://prelectur.stanford.edu/lecturers/bhabha/reviews.html [originally published in *Artforum* 33:7 (1995): 80-84] (accessed June 18, 2007). See also Jonathan Rutherford, "The Third Space: Interview with Homi Bhabha" in his *Identity: Community, Culture, Difference* (London: Lawrence and Wishart, 1990), 207-21 and Rubah Salih, "Shifting Boundaries of Self and Other; Moroccan Migrant Women in Italy," *European Journal of Women's Studies* 7 (2000): 321-35; Homi K. Bhabha, *The Location of Culture* (London: Routledge, 1994), 37.
3. On Islam and heavy metal, see the remarkable survey Mark LeVine, *Heavy Metal Islam: Rock, Resistance and the Struggle for the Soul of Islam* (New York: Three Rivers Press, 2008). See also Allegra Stratton, *Muhajababes: Meet the New Middle East – Cool, Sexy and Devout* (London: Constable, 2006).
4. I am aware of the limitations of using "Muslim" as a collective signifier of identity in this context: one of the authors to be considered – Courtauld – is a

Zoroastrian, and three others – Hirsi Ali, Djavann and Oufkir – while raised as Muslims, have renounced their faith. However, other terms are more problematic: "Arab" simply inaccurate, "Middle Eastern" too vague, "Oriental" too romantic and too externally imposed, and so on. In this essay, I will use "Muslim" in a loose, cultural sense, to denote someone who was born and educated in a Muslim-majority society, and who has resided there.

5. See Billie Melman, *Women's Orients: English Women and the Middle East, 1718-1918,* second edition (Houndsmill: MacMillan, 1995).

6. A claim put forward in Lila Azam Zanganeh, "Women without Men: A Conversation with Shirin Neshat" in *My Sister, Guard Your Veil; My Brother, Guard Your Eyes: Uncensored Iranian Voices*, ed. Lila Azam Zanganeh (Boston, Massachusetts: Beacon Press, 2006), 44-54.

7. "First Lady Laura Bush recommends…." The WHS Lions' Library, http://www.whslibrary.com/firstladyrecommends.htm (accessed August 18, 2009).

8. Farzaneh Milani, "On Women's Captivity in the Islamic World," *Merip* 246 (2008), http://www.merip.org/mer/mer246 (accessed December 10, 2008). I have found this work exceptionally useful.

9. All the following short quotes are taken from the "publisher's description" section for the relevant works on Amazon.co.uk and Amazon.com (accessed May 1, 2010).

10. My definition of Orientalism is drawn from the classic work by Edward Said, *Orientalism* (Harmondsworth: Penguin, 1978). While this work has been met with many criticisms and revision, its basic thesis that a distinctive western vision of Arab society evolved during the eighteenth and nineteenth centuries, that this vision was predicated on xenophobic vision, and that it assisted a colonizing drive seems indisputable.

11. Zainab Salbi (with Laurie Beckland), *Between Two Worlds: Escape into Tyranny; Growing Up in the Shadow of Saddam* (New York: Gotham, 2005), 190.

12. Nahal Tajadod, *Passeport à l'iranienne* (Paris: JC Lattès, 2007), 7; Carmen Bin Ladin, *The Veiled Kingdom* (London: Virago, 2004), 1; "Riverbend," *Baghdad Burning,* 31.

13. Sattareh Farman Farmaian with Donna Munker, *Daughter of Persia: A Woman's Journey from her Father's Harem through the Islamic Revolution* (London: Corgi, 1992), 11.

14. Nasrin Alavi, *We are Iran* (London: Portobello Books, 2005). This is an extremely useful edited collection of dissident texts from Iran. As it includes works by both men and women, it is only of peripheral interest to this paper.

15. The title is perhaps somewhat more pointed than my translation suggests: "An Iranian sort of passport" might be more accurate.

16. Pari Courtauld, *A Persian Childhood* (London: Rubicon Press, 1990), 25.

17. Carmen Bin Ladin, *The Veiled Kingdom* (London: Virago, 2004), 13, 61, 63.

18. Ayaan Hirsi Ali, *The Caged Virgin: A Muslim Woman's Cry for Reason* (London: Simon & Schuster, 2006), 5; Chahdortt Djavann, *Je viens d'ailleurs* (Paris: Autrement, 2002), 51.

19. Shirin Ebadi (with Azadeh Moaveni), *Iran Awakening: From Prison to Peace Prize: One Woman's Struggle at the Crossroads of History* (London: Rider, 2006), 53.
20. Azar Nafisi, *Reading Lolita in Tehran: A Memoir in Books* (New York: Random House, 2003), 261.
21. Veronica Doubleday, *Three Women of Herat* (London: Jonathan Cape, 1988), 2.
22. Christina Lamb, *The Sewing Circles of Herat; My Afghan Years* (London: HarperCollins, 2002), 216.
23. Bin Ladin, *Veiled Kingdom*, 206.
24. Hirsi Ali, *Caged Virgin*, 44.
25. Bin Ladin, *Veiled Kingdom*, 99. On the topic of Islam and modernity, see the fascinating study Christopher Houston, "The Brewing of Islamist Modernity: Tea Gardens and Public Space in Istanbul," *Theory, Culture and Society* 18:6 (2001): 77-97.
26. Kathleen Davis, "Time Behind the Veil: the Media, the Middle Ages and Orientalism Now" in *The Postcolonial Middle Ages,* ed. Jeffrey Jerome Cohen (Houndsmills: MacMillan, 2000), 105-22.
27. See the interesting comparative survey by Azadeh Kian-Thiébaut, "L'islam, les femmes et la citoyenneté," *Pouvoirs* 104 (2003): 71-84.
28. Bin Ladin, *Veiled Kingdom*, 9.
29. Ayaan Hirsi Ali, "I Will Continue to Ask Uncomfortable Questions", *Middle East Quarterly* (Fall 2006), http://www.meforum.org/1029/ayaan-hirsi-ali-i-will-continue-to-ask. (accessed June 6, 2008).
30. Malika Oufkir with Michele Fitoussi, *La Prisonnière*, trans., Ros Schwartz (London: Doubleday, 2000), 211, 235.
31. Tajadod, *Passeport*, 34 and 153-56.
32. "Riverbend," *Baghdad Burning*, 47.
33. Oufkir, *Prisonnière*, 29-31, 53.
34. Nafisi, *Reading Lolita*, 61 ; Djavann, *Je viens*, 57; Chahdortt Djavann, *Comment peut-on être français?* (Paris : Flammarion, 2006), 11.
35. Lamb, *Sewing Circles*, 158.
36. On this point, see Arjun Appadurai, *Modernity at Large: Cultural Dimensions of Globalization* (Minneapolis: University of Minnesota Press, 1996), 29-30; John Tomlinson "'Watching Dallas': the Imperialist Text and Audience Research" in *The Globalization Reader,* eds. Frank J. Lechner and John Boli (London: Blackwell, 2000), 307-15. Levine, *Heavy Metal Islam*, describes a far more complex process of exchange, interchange, synthesis and original creation.
37. Salbi, *Between Two Worlds*, 121.
38. Farmaian *Daughter of Persia*, 357, 377.
39. Ebadi, *Iran Awakening*, 33.
40. Ebadi, *Iran Awakening*, 61.
41. Salbi, *Between Two Worlds*, 13.
42. Tajadod, *Passeport*, 35-36.
43. Tajadod, *Passeport*, 117.

44. Tajadod, *Passeport*, 90.
45. Tajadod, *Passeport*, 112.
46. Saïda Rahal-Sidhoum, "Féministe et de culture musulmane dans la société française: une identité sans contrôle," (article posted 5 February 5 2007) MOUVEMENT des INDIGENES de la REPUBLIQUE, http://www.indigenes-republique.org/spip.php?article680 (accessed February 7, 2007).
47. Hirsi Ali, *Caged Virgin*, 29.
48. Tajadod, *Passeport*, 140.
49. Doubleday, *Three Women of Herat*, 3.
50. Doubleday, *Three Women of Herat*, 64-65. Another frustrating point in this description is that Doubleday never explains exactly what is meant by burqa and chador, and the reader therefore is never certain exactly what she is wearing.
51. "Riverbend," *Baghdad Burning*, 61- 62.
52. Rabineau, "Dévoilez Chahdortt," *Topo* 11 (November 2004): 26.
53. Gelareh Asayeh, "I Grew Up Thinking I was White" in *My Sister, Guard Your Veil; My Brother, Guard Your Eyes: Uncensored Iranian Voices*, ed. Lila Azam Zanganeh (Boston, Massachusetts: Beacon Press, 2006), 12-19.
54. Farmaian, *Daughter of Persia*, 225.
55. Marjane Satrapi, "How Can One Be Persian?" in *My Sister, Guard Your Veil; My Brother, Guard Your Eyes* 20-23.
56. Alavi, *We are Iran* (London: Portobello Books, 2005), 194.
57. "Riverbend," *Iran Awakening*, 122.
58. Salbi, *Between Two Worlds*, 214.
59. Salbi, *Between Two Worlds*, 191.
60. Salbi, *Between Two Worlds*, 204.
61. Salbi, *Between Two Worlds*, 208.
62. Salbi, *Between Two Worlds*, 267. For a fuller discussion of this point, see Chandra Talpade Mohanty, "'Under Western Eyes' Revisited: Feminist Solidarity through Anticapitalist Struggles," *Signs*, 28:2 (2002): 499-535.
63. Salbi, *BetweenTwo Worlds*, 290.
64. Milani, "On Women's Captivity."
65. Hirsi Ali, *Caged Virgin*, xvi.
66. See, for example, Jeremy Stolow, "Transnationalism and the New Religio-Politics: Reflections on a Jewish Orthodox Case," *Theory, Culture and Society* 21:2 (2004): 109-37 and Olivier Roy, *L'Islam Mondialisé* (Paris: Seuil, 2002).
67. John Hutnyk, "Hybridity," *Ethnic and Racial Studies* 28:1 (2005): 79-102. See also Jennier Yee, "Métissage in France: A Postmodern Fantasy and its Forgotten Precedents," *Modern and Contemporary France* 11:4 (2003): 411-26.

BIBLIOGRAPHIES

Katherine Holden and Fiona Reid, Introduction

Primary Sources

Archives of the International Red Cross, Geneva, G68 932 Otto Beilke, Comité Internationale de la Croix-Rouge, Genève, G68 932 February-April 1948.

McNeil, Margaret. *By the Rivers of Babylon: A Story Based upon Actual Experiences among the Displaced Persons of Europe*. Great Britain: Lincolnshire Chronicle, 1950.

UNRRA, *Helping the People to Help Themselves: The Story of the United Nations Relief and Rehabilitation Administration*. London: His Majesty's Stationery Office, 1944.

United Nations High Commission for Refugees (UNHCR) *2008 Global Trends: Refugees, Asylum-Seekers, Returnees, Internally Displaced and Stateless Persons* Country Data Sheets, 16 June 2009 http://www.unhcr.org/4a375c426.html

Secondary Sources

Anderson, Benedict. *Imagined Communities: Reflections on the Origin and Spread of Nationalism*. London: Verso, 1991.

Bessel, Richard and Haake, Claudia B. *Removing Peoples: Forced Removal in the Modern* World. Oxford: Oxford University Press, 2009.

Burrell, Kathy and Panayi, Panikos." Immigration, History and Memory in Britain." In *Histories and Memories: Migrants and their History in Britain*, edited by Kathy Burrell and Panikos Panayi, 3-18. London: Tauris Academic Studies, 2006.

Davis, Mike. *Late Victorian Holocausts*: *El Niño Famines and the Making of the Third* World. London: New York: Verso, 2001.

Gemie, Sharif, Humbert, Laure and Reid, Fiona "Shadow Double: Refugee and Citizen," *Planet: the Welsh Internationalist* 192 (December/January 2008-2009): 63-66.

Marrus, Michael R. "The Uprooted: An Historical Perspective." In *The Uprooted: Forced Migration as an International Problem in the Post-*

War Era, edited by Göran Rystad , 47-59. Lund: Lund University Press, 1990.

Pagden, Anthony. *Peoples and Empires: Europeans and the Rest of the World From Antiquity to the Present*. London: Phoenix, 2002.

Thackeray, William Makepeace. *Vanity Fair*. London: Penguin, 2003 [First published 1847-48].

Wyman, Mark. *DPs: Europe's Displaced Persons, 1945-1951*. Ithaca and London: Cornell University Press, 1998.

Raingard Esser, "Out of sight and on the margins? Migrating Women in Early Modern Europe"

Bade, Klaus. "Historische Migrationsforschung." In *Migration in der europäischen Geschichte seit dem späten Mittelalter* (IMIS Studien 20), edited by Klaus Bade, 21-44. Osnabrück: Universitätsverlag Rasch, 2003.

Bade, Klaus J. Emmer, Pieter C. Lucassen, Leo. Jochen, Oltmer. eds., *Enzyklopädie Migration in Europa vom 17. Jahrhundert bis zur Gegenwart.* Paderborn: Schöningh, 2007. [2nd edition 2008].

Boyd, Monica. "Family and Personal Networks in International Migration, Developments and New Agendas." *International Migration Review* 23 (1989): 689-671.

Brettell, Caroline B. "Theorizing Migration in Anthropology. The Social Construction of Networks, Identities, Communities and Globalspace." In *Migration Theory. Talking across Disciplines*, edited by Caroline B. Brettell, James Hollifield, 97-137. London: Routledge, 2000.

Bras, Hilde. "Maids to the City. Migration patterns of female domestic servants." *The History of the Family* 8 (2003): 217-246.

Chappell, Carolyn Lougee. "'The Pains I took to Save My/His Family': Escape Accounts by a Huguenot Mother and Daughter after the Revocation of the Edict of Nantes." *French Historical Studies* 22, 1 (1999): 1-64.

—. "'What's in a Name?': Self Identification of Huguenot *Réfugiées* in Eighteenth-Century England." In *From Strangers to Citizens: The Integration of Immigrant Communities in Britain, Ireland and Colonial America 1550-1750*, edited by Randolph Vigne and Charles Littleton, 539-548. London: Sussex Academic Press, 2001.

Choquette, Leslie. "'*Ces Amazones du Grand Dieu*': Women and Mission in Seventeenth Century Canada." *French Historical Studies* 17, 3 (1992): 627-655.

Datta, Satya. *Women and Men in Early Modern Venice*. Aldershot: Ashgate, 2003.

Davis, Natalie Zemon. "New Worlds, Marie de L'Incarnation." In *Women on the Margins. Three Seventeenth-Century Lives*, edited by Natalie Zemon Davis, 63-139. Cambridge/Mass.: Harvard University Press, 1995.

Dekker, Rudolf, Lotte van de Pol. *The Tradition of Female Transvestism in Early Modern Europe* Basingstoke: Palgrave MacMillan, 1989.

Esser, Raingard. "'Language no Obstacle'": War brides in the German Press, 1945-1949." *Women's History Review* 12, 4 (2003): 577-604.

François, Etienne. "Die Traditions- und Legendenbildung des deutschen Refuge." In *Der Exodus der Hugenotten. Die Aufhebung des Ediktes von Nantes 1685 als europäisches Ereignis*, edited by Heinz Duchhardt, 177-185. Cologne, Weimar, Vienna: Böhlau, 1985.

Gedenkbuch der Frau Maria Cordula Freiin von Pranck, verwitwete Hacke, geb. Radhaupt, 1595-1700, printed in: Steiermärkische Geschichtsblätter 2, 1881,H1, p. 2-29.

Geldsetzer, Sabine. *Fruven auf Kreuzzügen 1096-129.* Darmstadt: WBG, 2003.

Goose, Nigel and Lien. B. Luu. Introduction to *Immigrants in Tudor and Early Stuart England*, edited by Nigel Goose and Lien B. Luu, 1-40. Brighton: Sussex Academic Press, 2005.

Hagemann, Karen, "Militär, Krieg und Geschlechterverhältnisse. Untersuchungen, Überlegungen und Fragen zur Militärgeschichte der Frühen Neuzeit." In *Klio in Uniform? Probleme und Perspektiven einer modernen Militärgeschichte der Frühen Neuzeit,* edited by Ralf Pröve, 35-88. Cologne, Weimar, Vienna: Böhlau,1997.

Handlin, Oscar. *The Uprooted.* New York 1951.

Harzig, Christiane. "Women migrants as global and local agents. New research strategies on gender and migration." In *Women, Gender and Labour Migration: Historical and Global Perspectives*, edited by Pamela Sharpe, 15-28. London: Routledge, 2001.

Henry, Gráinne. "Women 'Wild Geese', 1585-1625: Irish Women and Migration to European Armies in the Late Sixteenth and Early Seventeenth Centuries." In *Irish Women and Irish Migration,* edited by Patrick O'Sullivan, 23-40. London: Leicester University Press, 1995.

Kloek, Els. "Vrouwenarbeid aan banden gelegd? De arbeidsdeling naar sekse volgens de keurboeken van de oude draperie van Leiden, ca. 1380-1580." *Tijdschrift voor Sociale Geschiedenis* 13 (1987): 373-402.

Knox, Andrea. "Women of the 'Wild Geese': Irish Women, Exile and Identity in Spain, 1750-1775." *Immigrants and Minorities* 23, 2-3 (2005): 143-159.

Kroener, Bernhard. "…'und ist der jammer nit zu beschreiben'. Geschlechterbeziehungen und Überlebensstrategien in der Lagergesellschaft des Dreißigjährigen Krieges." In *Landsknechte, Soldatenfrauen und Nationalkrieger. Militär und Geschlechterordnung im historischen Wandel*, edited by Karen Hagemann and Ralf Pröve, 279-297. Frankfurt: Campus Fachbuch,1998.

Kuijpers, Erika. *Migrantenstad. Immigratie en sociale verhoudingen in 17e eeuws Amsterdam.* Hilversum: Verloren, 2005.

Lenz, Ilse. Helma Lutz. Mirjana Morokvasic, Schöning-Kalenfar. Schwenken, Helen, eds. *Crossing borders, shifting boundaries, Vol. II, Gender and Networks*. Opladen: Leske und Budrich, 2002.

Lucassen, Jan. "Female migrations to Amsterdam. A response to Lotte van de Pol." In *Women of the Golden Age. An International Debate on Women in Seventeenth Century Holland, England and Italy*, edited by Els Kloek, Nicole Teeuwen, Marijke Huisman, 85. Hilversum: Verloren, 1994.

Lucassen, Leo. "Grensoverschrijding. Vrouwen en gender in historische migratiestudies." *Gaan & Staan. Jaarboek voor Vrouwengeschiedenis* (2001): 9-35.

Luu, Lien Bich. *Immigrants and the Industries of London, 1500-1700* Aldershot: Ashgate, 2005.

Maier, Christoph T. "The roles of women in the crusade movement: a survey." *Journal of Medieval History* 30, 1 (2004): 61-82.

Moens, William, John Charles. *The Walloons and their Church in Norwich.* 2 vols., Lymington: Huguenot Society of London Publications 1, 1887-1888.

Momsen, Janet Henshall, ed. *Gender, migration and domestic service.* London: Routledge, 1999.

Murdoch, Steve. *Network North. Scottish Kin, Commercial and Covert Associations in Northern Europe, 1603-1746.* Leiden, Boston: Brill, 2006.

O'Carroll, Ide B. "Breaking the silence from a distance: Irish women speak of sexual abuse." In *Irish Women and Irish Migration,* edited by Patrick O'Sullivan, 192-200. London: Leicester University Press, 1995.

Peters, Jan, ed. *Ein Söldnerleben im Dreißigjährigen Krieg. Eine Quelle zur Sozialgeschichte*. Berlin: Akademie Verlag, 1993.

van de Pol, Lotte. *Het Amsterdams Hoerdom, Prostitutie in de zeventiende en achttiende eeuw*. Amsterdam: Wereldbibliotheek, 1996.

van de Pol, Lotte and Erika Kuijpers. "Poor Women's Migration to the City: The Attraction of Amsterdam Health Care and Social Assistance in Early Modern Times." *Journal of Urban History* 32 (2005): 44-60.

Regtdoorzee Greup-Roldanus, S.C. "De vrouw in een oud-Hollandsch plattelandsbedrijf." In Fragmenten vrouwengeschiedenis, edited by W. Fritschy, Vol. 1. 44-56. The Hague: M.Nijhoff, 1980.

Rogg, Matthias. *Landsknechte und Reisläufer: Ein Stand in der Kunst des 16. Jahrhunderts*. Paderborn: Schöningh, 2002.

Rottloff, Andrea. *Stärker als Männer und tapferer als Ritter. Pilgerinnen in Spätantike und Mittelalter*. Mainz: Zabern, 2007.

Rublack, Ulinka. *The Crimes of Women in Early Modern Germany*. Oxford: Clarendon Press, 1999.

Sharpe, Pamela. "Introduction: Gender and the experience of migration." In *Women, Gender and Labour Migration: Historical and Global Perspectives*, edited by Pamela Sharpe, 1-14. London: Routledge, 2001.

Sinke, Suzanne S. "Gender and Migration: Historical Perspectives." *International Migration Review* 40, 1 (2006): 82-103.

Trim, David J.B. "Army, Society and Military Professionalism in the Netherlands during the Eighty Years' War." In *The Chivalric Ethos and the Development of Military Professionalism,* edited by David J.B. Trim, 269-291. Leiden, Boston: Brill, 2003).

Walker, Claire. *Gender and Politics in Seventeenth Century English Convents in France and the Low Countries*. Basingstoke: Palgrave MacMillan, 2003.

White, Ian D. *Migration and Society in Britain 1550-1830*. Basingstoke: Palgrave MacMillan, 2000.

Wunder, Heide. *'Er ist die Sonn', sie ist der Mond'. Frauen in der Frühen Neuzeit*. Munich: Beck, 1992.

Young, Francis. "Mother Mary More and the Exile of the Augustinian Canonesses of Bruges in England, 1794-1802." *Recusant History* 27/1 (2004): 86-102.

Virginia Bainbridge, "Propaganda and the Supernatural: The Bridgettine Nuns of Syon Abbey in Exile c. 1539-1630"

Unpublished Primary Sources

British Library (BL)
BL, Add. MS. 22285, Syon Abbey Martiloge
BL, Add. MS. 18650, The Life and Good End of Sr Marie
Exeter University Library (EUL)
EUL, MS. 95, Canon John Rory Fletcher's mss.
EUL, Syon Abbey unnumbered MS: 'English Saintes of Kinges and Bishoppes in the primitive times of the Catholique church…'

Primary Printed and Secondary sources (* for Primary Printed)

Anstruther, Geoffrey. *A Hundred Homeless Years: English Dominicans* 1558-1658. London: Blackfriars, 1958.

Aungier, George J. *The History and Antiquities of Syon Monastery, Isleworth*. London: J.B. Nichols, 1840.

Bainbridge, Virginia R. "Women and the Transmission of Religious Culture: benefactresses of three Bridgettine convents" *Birgittiana* 1 (1997): 55-76.

—. "The Bridgettines and Major Trends in Religious Devotion *c.* 1400-1600", *Birgittiana* 19 (2005): 225-240.

—. "Who were the English Birgittines? The brothers and sisters of Syon Abbey 1415-1600." In *Saint Birgitta, Syon and Vadstena,* edited by Claes Gejrot, Sara Risburg and Mia Äkestam, 37-49. Stockholm: Kungl. Vitterhets Historie och Antikvitets Akademien, 2010.

—. "Women and Learning: Syon Abbey c. 1415-1600." In *Syon Abbey and its Books c. 1400-1700,* edited by Edward A. Jones, and Alexandra M. Walsham, 82-103. Woodbridge, Suffolk: Boydell and Brewer, 2010.

* *Calendar of Letters & Papers, Foreign and Domestic, of the Reign of Henry VIII* (London: HMSO, 1864-1932)

Challoner, Richard. *Memoirs of Missionary Priests* 1577-1684, revised editon. London: Burns and Oates, 1924.

* Chauncy, Maurice. *Historia Aliquot Martyrum Anglorum.* London: Burns and Oates, 1888.

* Clifford, Henry. *The Life of Jane Dormer, Duchess of Feria*, translated by E.E. Estcourt, edited by J. Stevenson. London: Burns and Oates, 1887.

Cokayne, George E. and Gibbs, Vicary eds., *The Complete Peerage,* 12 vols. London: 2nd. edition, St Catherine Press, 1910-59.

Davidson, A. "Roman Catholicism in Oxfordshire c. 1580-1640." PhD diss, University of Bristol, 1970.

Dillon, Anne. *The Construction of Martyrdom in the English Catholic Community* 1535-1603. Oxford: University of Oxford Press, 2003.

Donnet, F. "Les Brigittines Anglaises à Mishagen," *Annales du Congrès Historique et Archéologique de Malines* 2 (1911): 55-63.

Dowling, Maria. "Humanist support for Katherine of Aragon," *Bulletin of the Institute of Historical Research* 57 (1984): 46-55.

* Dowling, Maria. ed., "William Latymer's Chronickille of Anne Bulleyne," *Camden Miscellany* 30, 4th series, 39. London: Royal Historical Society, 1990, 23-65

Fletcher, John Rory. *The Story of the English Bridgettines.* South Brent, Devon: Syon Abbey, 1933.

* Gee, J. *New Shreds of the old Snare, containing the apparitions of two new female ghosts etc.* London: printed by John Dawson for Robert Milbourne, 2nd edition, 1624.

Guilday, Peter *The English Catholic Refugees on the Continent 1558-1795.* London: Longman, 1914.

* de. Hamel, C. ed., *Syon Abbey, the Library of the Bridgettine Nuns & their Peregrinations after the Reformation.* London: Roxburgh Club, 1991.

Hamilton, Adam. *The Angel of Syon: the Life and Martyrdom of the Blessed Richard Reynolds.* Edinburgh: Sands, 1905.

* Hutchison Ann M., ed., "Mary Champney a Bridgettine nun under the rule of Queen Elizabeth I", *Birgittiana* 13 (2002).

Hutchison, Ann M. "Beyond the Margins: the Recusant Bridgettines." In *Studies in St Birgitta and the Brigittine Order*, edited by J. Hogg, 2, 267-84. Salzburg: *Analecta Cartusiana* 35:19, 1993.

—. "Syon Abbey: Dissolution, no Decline", *Birgittiana* 2 (1996): 245-59.

—. "Syon Abbey Preserved: some Historians of Syon." In *Syon Abbey and its Books c. 1400-1700,* edited by Edward A. Jones, and Alexandra M. Walsham, 228-51.Woodbridge, Suffolk: Boydell and Brewer, 2010.

Johnston, Francis R. *Syon Abbey.* Eccles: Eccles and District History Society, 1964.

Johnson, Trevor. "Blood, Tears and Xavier Water: Jesuit Missionaries and Popular Religion." In *Popular Religion in Germany and Central*

Europe 1400-1800, edited by Bob Scribner and Trevor Johnson, 183-202. London: Macmillan, 1996.

Jones, Edward A. and Walsham Alexandra M., eds. *Syon Abbey and its Books c. 1400-1700*. Woodbridge, Suffolk: Boydell and Brewer, 2010.

Knowles, David. *The Religious Orders in England*, 3 vols. Cambridge: University of Cambridge Press, 1955-59.

* Knox, T.F. ed., *Records of the English Catholics under the Penal Laws*. London: David Nutt, 1878.

Lechat, R. "Une Communauté Anglaise réfugiée à Malines au XVIe Siècle: Les Brigittines de Sion" *Annales du Congrès Historique et Archéologique Malines*, 2 (1911): 243-59

Marshall, Peter. *Beliefs and the Dead in Reformation England*. Oxford: University of Oxford Press, 2002.

Morris, Bridget. *St Birgitta of Sweden*. Woodbridge, Suffolk: Boydell, 1999.

* Morris J. ed. *The Troubles of our Catholic Forefathers* 3 vols. London: Burns and Oates, 1872-77.

Neame, Alan. *The Holy Maid of Kent: the Life of Elizabeth Barton 1506-1534*. London: Hodder and Stoughton, 1971.

The Oxford Dictionary of National Biography http://www.oxforddnb.com

Questier, Michael. *Catholicism and Community in Early Modern England*. Cambridge: Cambridge University Press, 2006.

Redworth, Glyn. *The Prince and the Infanta*. New Haven: University of Yale Press, 2003.

Redworth, Glyn *The She-Apostle*. Oxford: University of Oxford Press, 2008.

* Robinson, Thomas. *Anatomy of the English Nunnery at Lisbon*. London, 1622.

* de. Vlaminck, A. ed., *L'Église Collegiale Nôtre Dame à Termonde et son ancien Obituaire*. Termonde: Cercle Archéologique de la ville et de l'ancien pays de Termonde, Termonde 1898.

Walker, Claire. *Gender and Politics in Early Modern Europe: English Convents in France and the Low Countries*. Basingstoke: Palgrave, 2003.

—. "Continuity and Isolation: the Bridgettines of Syon in the Sixteenth and Seventeenth Centuries." In *Syon Abbey and its Books c. 1400-1700,* edited by Edward A. Jones, and Alexandra M. Walsham, 155-76. Woodbridge, Suffolk: Boydell and Brewer, 2010.

Walsham, Alexandra. "Miracles and the Counter-Reformation Mission to England." *Historical Journal* 46 (2003): 779-815.

Katy Gibbons, "'An Unquiet Estate Abroad': The Religious Exile of Catholic Noblewomen and Gentlewomen under Elizabeth I"

Unpublished Primary Sources

The National Archives, London, Prerogative Court of Canterbury, PROB 11

—. State Papers Domestic, SP 12

—. State Papers Domestic Addenda, SP 15

—. State Papers Scotland, SP 52

North Yorkshire County Record Office, Northallerton, ZS Swinton Estate and Middleham Estate Records

Printed Primary Sources

Calendar of State Papers, Domestic Series in the Reigns of Elizabeth and James I, Addenda, 1580-1625, ed. Mary Anne Everett Green (London: H.M.S.O., 1872)

A Collection of State Papers Relating to Affairs in the Reign of Queen Elizabeth, ed. William Murdin (London: William Bowyer, 1759)

Continuation des choses plus célèbres & memorables advenues en Angleterre, Escosse et Irlande (Lyon, 1570)

Discours des troubles nouellement aduenuz en Angleterre au moys d'octobre 1569 (Lyon, 1570)

"The Douay College Diaries, Third, Fourth and Fifth: 1598-1654", ed. Edwin H. Burton, *Catholic Record Society*, 11 (1911)

The First and the Second Diaries of the English College, Douay, ed. Thomas Francis Knox (London: D. Nutt, 1969)

Letters of Sir Thomas Copley, ed. Richard Copley Christie (London: Roxburghe Club, 1897)

"Letters of William Allen and Richard Barrett, 1572-1598", ed. P. Renold, *Catholic Record Society*, 58 (1996)

"Miscellanea Recusant Records", ed. Clare Talbot, *Catholic Record Society*, 53 (1960)

"Miscellanea I", ed. J. H. Pollen, *Catholic Record Society*, 1 (1905)

North Country Wills, Vol. II', *Surtees Society*, 121 (1912)

Norton, Thomas, *To the Quenes Maiesties poore deceived subiects of the northe contreye* (1569)

The Statutes of the Realm, 11 vols. (London: Dawsons, 1963)

Secondary Sources

Allen, Elizabeth. "John Copley." In *The Oxford Dictionary of National Biography*, edited by H. C. G. Matthew and Brian Harrison, 60 vols. 13: 342-343. Oxford: Oxford University Press, 2004.

Bossy, J.A. "Elizabethan Catholicism: The Link with France." PhD diss., University of Cambridge, 1960.

Bossy, John. *The English Catholic Community, 1570-1880.* London: Darton, Longman and Todd, 1975.

Bowden, Caroline M. K. "Lady Mary Percy." In *The Oxford Dictionary of National Biography*, edited by H.C. G. Matthew and Brian Harrison, 60 vols. 43: 734. Oxford: Oxford University Press, 2004.

Busse, Daniella, "Anti-Catholic Polemical Writing on the 'Rising in the North' (1569) and the Catholic Reaction." *Recusant History* 27 (2004): 11-30.

Caraman, Philip. *The Other Face: Catholic Life under Elizabeth I.* London: Longmans, 1960.

Davidoff, Leonore. "Gender and the 'Great Divide': Public and Private in British Gender History." *Journal of Women's History* 15 (2003): 11-27.

Dillon, Anne. *The Construction of Martyrdom in the English Catholic Community, 1535-1603*. Aldershot: Ashgate 2002.

Freeman, Thomas. "'The Good Ministrie of Godly and Virtuouse Women': The Elizabethan Martyrologists and the Female Supporters of Marian Martyrs." *Journal of British Studies* 39 (2000): 8-33.

Pettegree, Andrew, Malcolm Walsby, Alexander Wilkinson, eds. *French Vernacular Books: Books Published in the French language before 1601*. 2 vols. Leiden: Brill, 2007.

Gibbons, Katy. *English Catholics and Exile: Elizabethan Catholics in Paris.* (forthcoming)

Graves, Michael A. R. "Anthony Copley." In *The Oxford Dictionary of National Biography*, edited by H. C. G. Matthew and Brian Harrison, 60 vols. 13:342-343. Oxford: Oxford University Press, 2004.

Graves, Michael A. R."Thomas Copley." In *The Oxford Dictionary of National Biography*, edited by H. C. G. Matthew, and Brian Harrison, 60 vols. 13: 358-359. Oxford: Oxford University Press, 2004.

Hicks, Michael. "Richard Norton." In *The Oxford Dictionary of National Biography*, edited by H. C. G. Matthew and Brian Harrison, 60 vols. 41: 182-183. Oxford: Oxford University Press, 2004.

James, Mervyn. *Family, Lineage and Civil Society: a study of Society, Politics and Mentality in the Durham Region, 1500-1640*. Oxford: Clarendon Press 1974.

Kesselring, K. J. "'A Cold Pye for the Papistes': Constructing and Containing the Northern Rising of 1569." *Journal of British Studies* 43 (2004): 417-43.

—. *Mercy and Authority in the Tudor State*. Cambridge: Cambridge University Press, 2003.

Kesselring, Krista. *The Northern Rebellion of 1569: Faith, Politics and Protest in Elizabethan England*. Basingstoke: Palgrave Macmillan, 2007.

Lechat, Robert. *Les Réfugiés Anglais dans les Pays-Bays Espagnols durant le règne d'Élisabeth 1558-1603*. Louvain: Bureau de Recueils, 1914.

Lee, Sidney. "Thomas Percy." In *Dictionary of National Biography*, edited by Leslie Stephen and Sidney Lee, 22 vols. 15:878-81. London: Oxford University Press, 1885-1900.

Lock, Julian. "Thomas Percy." In *The Oxford Dictionary of National Biography*, edited by H. C. G. Matthew and Brian Harrison, 60 vols. 43:740-45. Oxford: Oxford University Press, 2004.

Loomie, A. J. *The Spanish Elizabethans: the English Exiles at the Court of Philip II*. London: Burns and Oates, 1963.

Lowers, James K. *Mirrors for Rebels: a study of Polemical Literature relating to the Northern Rebellion, 1569*. Berkeley: University of California Press, 1953.

MacCulloch, Diarmaid. *Reformation: Europe's House Divided, 1490-1700*. London: Penguin, 2003.

Magnusson, Lynne. "A Rhetoric of Requests: Genre and Linguistic Scripts in Elizabethan Women's Suitors' Letters." In *Women and Politics in Early Modern England (1450-1700)*, edited by James Daybell, 58-64. Aldershot: Ashgate, 2004.

Marshall, Peter. "Exiles and the Tudor State," In *Discipline and Diversity*, edited by Kate Cooper and Jeremy Gregory, 43, 263-284. Woodbridge: Ecclesiastical History Society/Boydell Press, 2007.

Marshall, Peter. "'The Greatest Man in Wales:' James ap Gruffydd ap Hywel and the International Opposition to Henry VIII." *Sixteenth Century Journal* 39 (2008): 681-704.

Merrick, M. M. *Thomas Percy, Seventh Earl*. London: Duckett, 1949.

Neale, J. E. *Elizabeth I and her Parliaments 1584-1601*. London: Cape, 1957.

Proost, J. J. E. "Les Réfugiés Anglais et Irlandais en Belgique, à la suite de la Réforme religieuse établie sous Élizabeth et Jacques Ier." *Messager des Sciences Historiques* (1865): 277-314.

Questier, Michael. *Catholicism and Community in Early Modern England: Politics, Aristocratic Patronage and Religion, c. 1550-1640.* Cambridge: Cambridge University Press, 2006.

Rowlands, Marie B. "Harbourers and Housekeepers: Catholic Women in England, 1570-1720." In *Catholic Communities in Protestant States*, edited by Benjamin J. Kaplan, Bob Moore, Henk Van Nierop and Judith Pollmann, 200- 215. Manchester: Manchester University Press, 2009.

—. "Recusant Women 1560-1640." In *Women in English Society 1500-1800*, edited by Mary Prior, 153-54. London: Routledge, 1985.

Ryrie, Alec. *The Gospel and Henry VIII: Evangelicals in the early English Reformation.* Cambridge: Cambridge University Press 2003.

Sharp, Cuthbert. *Memorials of the Rebellion of 1569.* London: J. B. Nichols and Son, 1840.

Somerset, Anne. *Elizabeth I.* London: St Martin's Press, 1992.

Taylor, Susan E. "The Crown and the North of England, 1559-70: A study of the Rebellion of the Northern Earls 1569-70 and its Causes." PhD diss., University of Manchester, 1981.

Vickery, Amanda. "Golden Age to Separate Spheres: A Review of the Categories and Chronology of English Women's History." *Historical Journal* 36 (1993): 383-414.

Walker, Clare. "Dorothy Lawson." In *The Oxford Dictionary of National Biography*, edited by H. C. G. Matthew and Brian Harrison, 60 vols. 32: 883-84. Oxford: Oxford University Press, 2004.

—. *Gender and Politics in Early Modern Europe: English Convents in France and the Low Countries.* Basingstoke: Palgrave Macmillan, 2003.

Evelyn Kassouf Spratt, "*Française* or American?: The Immigration Story of Josephine du Pont, 1795 to 1833"

Unpublished Primary Sources

Correspondence between Madame Victor Marie du Pont and Madame Manigault. Accession #502. Hagely Museum and Library. Delaware.

Du Pont, Josephine. *Souvenirs de Madame Victor Marie du Pont de Nemours.* DE: Printed Privately. 1908.

—. "Notre transplantation en Amérique." translated by Sophie du Pont. Accession #502. Hagely Museum and Library. Delaware.

Papers of Gabrielle Josephine de la Fite de Pellport. Winterthur Manuscripts. Group 3, Series D. Hagely Museum and Library. Delaware.

Papers of Victor Marie du Pont. Winterthur Manuscripts. Group 3, Series A, B and C. Hagely Museum and Library. Delaware.

Secondary Sources

Altman, Ida, and James Horn. *To Make America: European Emigration in the Early Modern Period.* Berkeley, Oxford: University of California Press, 1991.

Baesler, Marylin. *"Asylum for Mankind," America, 1607- 1800.* New York: Cornell University Press, 1998.

Bailyn, Bernard. *The Peopling of North America*. New York: Knopf, 1986.

Boydston, Jeanne. "Making Gender in the Early Republic." In *The Revolution of 1800,* edited by James Horn, Jan Lewis and Peter Onuf, 240-266. Charlottesville: University of Virginia Press, 2002.

Chappell, Carolyn Lougee. "The Pains I Took to Save My/His Family: Escape Accounts by a Huguenot Mother and Daughter after the Revocation of Nantes." *French Historical Studies* 22/1 (Winter, 1999): 1-65.

Childs, Francis, S. *French Refugee Life in the United States, 1790-1800: An American Chapter of the French Revolution.* Baltimore: Johns Hopkins Press, 1940.

Echeverria, Durand. *Mirage in the West: A History of the French Image of American Society to 1815.* New York: Octagon Books, Inc. 1966.

Greer, Donald. *The Incidence of the Emigration during the French Revolution*. Cambridge, Mass.: Harvard University Press, 1951.

Hébert, C. "The Pennsylvania French in the 1790s: The story of their Survival." PhD. diss., University of Texas at Austin, 1980.

Kerber, Linda. "The Paradox of Women's Citizenship in the Early Republic: The Case of Martin vs. Massachusetts, 1805." In *Toward an Intellectual History of Women*, edited by Linda Kerber, 261-302. Chapel Hill, NC: University of North Carolina Press, 1997.

Kerber, Linda. "The Republican Mother: Women and the Enlightenment – An American Perspective." In *Toward an Intellectual History of Women*, edited by Linda Kerber, 41-62. Chapel Hill, NC: University of North Carolina Press, 1997.

Low, Betty-Bright, P. "Of Muslims and Merveilleuses: Excerpts from the Letters of Josephine du Pont and Margaret Manigault." *Winterthur Portfolio* 9 (1974): 24 – 75.

—. *France Views America: 1765-1815, An Exhibition to Commemorate the Bicentenary of French Assistance in the American War for Independence*. Wilmington: Elutherian Mills – Hagely Foundation, 1978.

Meadows, Darrell, R. "Engineering Social Networks and the French Atlantic Community, 1789-1809." *French Historical Studies* 23/1 (Winter, 2000): 68 -102.

Peterson, Linda, H. *The Traditions of Victorian Women's Autobiography.* Charlottesville: University of Virginia Press, 1999.

Wokeck, Marianne. *Trade in Strangers: The Beginning of Mass Migration to North America.* University Park: Pennsylvania State University Press, 1999.

Linda Martz, "Moved to Minister: Christabel Pankhurst and Aimee Semple McPherson in Los Angeles"

Primary sources

Aikman, Duncan. "California Sunshine." *The Nation* 132, April 22, 1931, 448.

Bliven, Bruce. "City that is Bacchanalian in a Nice Way." *New Republic* 51, July 13 1927, 197-200.

Comstock, Sarah. "The Great American Mirror: Reflections from Los Angeles." *Harper's Monthly* 156, May 1928, 715-723.

MacWilliams, Carey. *Southern California: An Island on the Land.* Salt Lake City: Peregrine Smith Books, 1990, reprint, [first published 1946]

McPherson, Aimee Semple. *This is That*. Los Angeles: Foursquare Publications, reprint 1996, [first published 1919.]

—. *In Service to the King*. Los Angeles: Foursquare Publications, reprint 1988, [first published 1927.]

—. *Aimee: Life Story of Aimee Semple McPherson*, Los Angeles: Foursquare Publications,1979.

Pankhurst, Christabel. *'The Lord Cometh': The World Crisis Explained.* London: Morgan & Scott, 1923.

—. *The World's Unrest: Visions of the Dawn*. London: Morgan and Scott, 1921.

Symes, Lillian. "The Beautiful and Dumb." *Harper's Monthly* 163, June 1931, 22-23.

Torrey, Reuben Archer. *The Fundamentals.* Grand Rapids, Michigan: Baker Books, 2003, [first published 1909.]

Voices of History: Historic Recordings from the British Library Sound Archive. The British Library Board, 2004.

West, Nathaniel. *Day of the Locust*. USA: Penguin Signet Classic, 1983, [first published 1939.]

Whitaker, Alma. "Christabel in Placid Role", *Los Angeles Times*, November 28, 1921, II3.

—. "Sugar and Spice," *Los Angeles Times*, August 8, 1943, D8.

Woelhke, Walter V. "Los Angeles – Homeland." *Sunset Magazine* (January 1911): 3-16.

—. "How Long, Los Angeles?" *Sunset Magazine* (April 1924): 8-11, 100-102.

Secondary sources

Blumhofer Edith L *Aimee Semple McPherson: Everybody's sister.* Grand Rapids, MI: William B. Eerdmans Publishing, 1993.

—. "Azusa Street Revival." *Christian Century* 123, 5 (7 March 2006): 20-22.

Bruce, Steve. *Fundamentalism.* Cambridge: Polity Press, 2000.

Engh, Michael E. "Practically Every Religion Being Represented." In *Metropolis in the Making: Los Angeles in the 1920s*, edited by Tom Sitton and William Deverell, 201-219 (Berkeley and Los Angeles: University of California Press).

Epstein, Daniel Mark. *Sister Aimee: The Life of Aimee Semple McPherson.* New York and London: Harcourt Brace Jovanovich, 1993.

Fogelson, Robert M. *The Fragmented Metropolis: Los Angeles 1850-1930.* Berkeley and Los Angeles: University of California Press, 1993.

Goff, Philip. "Fighting Like the Devil in the City of Angels: the Rise of Fundamentalist Charles E. Fuller." In *Metropolis in the Making: Los Angeles in the 1920s*, edited by Tom Sitton and William Deverell , 220 - 252 (Berkeley and Los Angeles: University of California Press).

Larsen, Timothy. *Christabel Pankhurst: Fundamentalism and Feminism in Coalition.* Woodbridge: The Boydell Press, 2002.

Marsden, George M. *Fundamentalism and American Culture.* Oxford: Oxford University Press, 2006.

Mitchell, David. *Queen Christabel.* London: MacDonald and Jane's, 1977.

Starr, Kevin. *Embattled Dreams: California in War and Peace 1940-1950.* Oxford: Oxford University Press, 2002.

Sutton, Matthew Avery, *Aimee Semple McPherson and the Resurrection of Christian America.* Cambridge MA: Harvard University Press, 2007.

Whacker, Grant. *Heaven Below: Early Pentecostals and American Culture.* Cambridge MA and London: Harvard University Press, 2001.

Zimmerman, Tom. *Paradise Promoted: The Booster Campaign that Created Los Angeles 1870-1930.* Los Angeles: Angel City Press, 2008.

Sharif Gemie, "Women, Exile and Islam"

Alavi, Nasrin. *We are Iran.* London: Portobello Books, 2005.

Appadurai, Arjun. *Modernity at Large: Cultural Dimensions of Globalization.* Minneapolis: University of Minnesota Press, 1996.

Asayeh, Gelareh. "I Grew Up Thinking I was White". In *My Sister, Guard Your Veil; My Brother, Guard Your Eyes: Uncensored Iranian Voices* edited by Lila Azam Zanganeh, 12-19. Boston, Massachusetts: Beacon Press, 2006.

Bhabha, Homi K. *The Location of Culture*. London: Routledge, 1994.

Bin Laden, Carmen. *The Veiled Kingdom.* London: Virago, 2004.

Courtauld, Pari. *A Persian Childhood.* London: Rubicon Press, 1990.

Davis, Kathleen. "Time Behind the Veil: the Media, the Middle Ages and Orientalism Now". In *The Postcolonial Middle Ages*, edited by Jeffrey Jerome Cohen, 105-22. Houndsmills: MacMillan, 2000.

Djavann, Chahdortt. *Je viens d'ailleurs.* Paris: Autrement, 2002.

—. *Comment peut-on être français?* Paris: Flammarion, 2006.

Doubleday, Veronica. *Three Women of Herat.* London: Jonathan Cape, 1988.

Ebadi, Shirin, with Azadeh Moaveni. *Iran Awakening: From Prison to Peace Prize: One Woman's Struggle at the Crossroads of History.* London: Rider, 2006.

Farmaian, Sattareh Farman, with Donna Munker. *Daughter of Persia: A Woman's Journey from her Father's Harem through the Islamic Revolution.* London: Corgi, 1992.

"First Lady Laura Bush Recommends...", WHS Lions' Library. http://www.whslibrary.com/firstladyrecommends.htm

Hirsi Ali, Ayaan. *The Caged Virgin: A Muslim Woman's Cry for Reason.* London: Simon & Schuster, 2006.

—. "I Will Continue to Ask Uncomfortable Questions." *Middle East Quarterly* (Fall 2006), http://www.meforum.org/1029/ayaan-hirsi-ali-i-will-continue-to-ask.

Houston, Christopher. "The Brewing of Islamist Modernity: Tea Gardens and Public Space in Istanbul." *Theory, Culture and Society* 18:6 (2001): 77-97.

Hutnyk, John. "Hybridity." *Ethnic and Racial Studies* 28:1 (2005): 79-102.

Kian-Thiébaut, Azadeh, "L'islam, les femmes et la citoyenneté." *Pouvoirs* 104 (2003): 71-84.

Lamb, Christina. *The Sewing Circles of Herat; My Afghan Years.* London: HarperCollins, 2002.

LeVine, Mark. *Heavy Metal Islam: Rock, Resistance and the Struggle for the Soul of Islam.* New York: Three Rivers Press, 2008.

Melman, Billie. *Women's Orients: English Women and the Middle East, 1718-1918*, second edition. Houndsmill: MacMillan, 1995.

Milani, Farzaneh. "On Women's Captivity in the Islamic World," *Middle East Report* 246 (2008), http://www.merip.org/mer/mer246/milani.html.

Mitchell, W. T. J. "Translator translated (interview with cultural theorist Homi Bhabha)", http://prelectur.stanford.edu/lecturers/bhabha/reviews.html [originally published in *Artforum* 33:7 (1995): 80-84] .

Oufkir, Malika with Michele Fitoussi, *La Prisonnière*, translated by Ros Schwartz. London: Doubleday, 2000.

Rabineau, Isabelle. "Dévoilez Chahdortt," *Topo* 11 (2004): 19-29.

Rahal-Sidhoum, Saïda. "Féministe et de culture musulmane dans la société française: une identité sans contrôle." Article posted 5 February, 2007, MOUVEMENT des INDIGENES de la REPUBLIQUE.. (http://www.indigenes-republique.org/spip.php?article680).

"Riverbend," *Baghdad Burning: Girl Blog from Iraq*. London: Marion Boyars, 2006.

Roy, Olivier. *L'Islam Mondialisé*. Paris: Seuil, 2002.

Rutherford, Jonathan. "The Third Space: Interview with Homi Bhabha". In his *Identity: Community, Culture, Difference* (London: Lawrence and Wishart, 1990), 207-21.

Said, Edward. *Orientalism*. Harmondsworth: Penguin, 1978.

Salbi, Zainab, with Laurie Beckland. *Between Two Worlds: Escape into Tyranny; Growing Up in the Shadow of Saddam*. New York: Gotham, 2005.

Salih, Rubah. "Shifting Boundaries of Self and Other; Moroccan Migrant Women in Italy." *European Journal of Women's Studies* 7 (2000): 321-35

Satrapi, Marjane. "How Can One Be Persian?" In *My Sister, Guard Your Veil; My Brother, Guard Your Eyes: Uncensored Iranian Voices* edited by Lila Azam Zanganeh, 20-23. Boston, Massachusetts: Beacon Press, 2006.

Stolow, Jeremy. "Transnationalism and the New Religio-Politics: Reflections on a Jewish Orthodox Case." *Theory, Culture and Society* 21:2 (2004): 109-37

Stratton, Allegra. *Muhajababes: meet the new Middle East – cool, sexy and devout.* London: Constable, 2006.

Mohanty, Chandra Talpade. "'Under Western Eyes' Revisited: Feminist Solidarity through Anticapitalist Struggles." *Signs*, 28:2 (2002): 499-535.

Nafisi, Azar. *Reading Lolita in Tehran: A Memoir in Books.* New York: Random House, 2003.

Tajadod, Nahal. *Passeport à l'iranienne.* Paris: JC Lattès, 2007.

Tomlinson, John. "'Watching Dallas': the Imperialist Text and Audience Research". In *The Globalization Reader* edited by Frank J. Lechner and John Boli, 307-15. London: Blackwell, 2000.

Yee, Jennifer. "Métissage in France: a postmodern fantasy and its forgotten precedents." *Modern and Contemporary France* 11:4 (2003): 411-26.

Zanganeh, Lila Azam. "Women without Men: A Conversation with Shirin Neshat." In *My Sister, Guard Your Veil; My Brother, Guard Your Eyes: Uncensored Iranian Voices* edited by Lila Azam Zanganeh, 44-54. Boston, Massachusetts: Beacon Press, 2006.

CONTRIBUTORS

Dr. Virginia Bainbridge, editor of the Victoria County History of Wiltshire at the University of the West of England, Bristol, England.

Dr. Raingard Esser, Reader in Early Modern History, the University of the West of England, Bristol, England.

Sharif Gemie, Professor in Modern and Contemporary History, University of Glamorgan, Wales.

Dr Katy Gibbons, Senior Lecturer in History, University of Portsmouth, England.

Dr Katherine Holden, Senior Lecturer in History, E-Learning and blended learning at the University of the West of England, Bristol, England.

Dr. Evelyn Kassouf Spratt, Assistant Professor, the College of Notre Dame of Maryland, Baltimore, Maryland, USA.

Dr. Linda Martz, Associate Professor of English and History, American University of Paris, France.

Dr Fiona Reid, Senior Lecturer in European History, University of Glamorgan, Wales.

NOTES ON EDITORS

Katherine Holden is a senior lecturer in history, e-learning and blended learning at the University of the West of England in Bristol. She is a founder member and treasurer of the West of England and South Wales Women's History Network and has also been an active member of the UK Women's History Network over the past two decades. She served on the steering committee of the UK network between 1997-2001, hosting the annual conference in Bath in 2000, and again from 2006 when she became Network Convenor and judge of the Claire Evans Prize. Some key publications in women's and gender history are: *The Shadow of Marriage: Singleness in England 1914-1960* (Manchester: Manchester University Press, 2007), *The Family Story: Blood, Contract and Intimacy 1830-1960*, co-authored with Leonore Davidoff, Megan Doolittle and Janet Fink, (Harlow, Essex: Longman, 1999), "Imaginary widows: spinsters, marriage and the 'lost generation' in Britain after the Great War" *Journal of Family History* 30/4, (2005):134-48 and "'Nature takes no notice of Morality': singleness, and Married Love in interwar Britain", *Women's History Review* 11/3 (2002): 481-503. Her current research project on the history of nannies in Britain will focus partly on the global dimensions of this form of employment, including the movement of women between cultures and across local and national boundaries.

Fiona Reid is a senior lecturer in European history at the University of Glamorgan. She is the secretary of the West of England and South Wales Women's History Network and she sits on the committee of the National Army Records Society. She has published widely on the social history of war in the twentieth century and is the author of *Broken Men: Shell Shock, Treatment and Recovery in Britain 1914-30* (Hambeldon Continuum: 2010). She is currently part of "Outcast Europe," a research centre funded by the Leverhulme Trust and based at the University of Glamorgan, and she is working on the history of displacement during the long Second World War. Her forthcoming work (with Sharif Gemie and Laure Humbert) is *Outcast Europe: 1936-1948* which will be published by Hambledon Continuum in 2011.

INDEX